The Metaverse Handbook

The Metaverse Handbook

Innovating for the Internet's Next Tectonic Shift

QuHarrison Terry
Scott "DJ SKEE" Keeney

WILEY

In memory of Jo Ann Shary and Linda Pittman

About the Authors

QuHarrison Terry is the bestselling author of *The NFT Handbook*, a detailed guide on how to create, sell, and buy nonfungible tokens without the need for a technical background. His work has been translated into more than seven languages and has appeared everywhere from WIRED to *Forbes*. In addition, QuHarrison is a four-time recipient of LinkedIn's Top Voices in Technology award.

QuHarrison is also a notable entrepreneur and growth marketer who has advised Mark Cuban and his portfolio of 200+ venture companies. He is the cohost of CNBC's primetime series *No Retreat: Business Bootcamp*. In 2022, he launched Metaverse QT.com, a website devoted to helping innovators and creative professionals understand the Metaverse.

Scott "DJ SKEE" Keeney has built an empire by consistently identifying the next trends in music and culture.

As a DJ, Skee is best known for introducing the world to artists including Kendrick Lamar, Lady Gaga, Post Malone, Travis Scott, and more on his TV and radio platforms. Skee has produced for defining artists of this era ranging from Snoop Dogg to Michael Jackson and composed music for top-selling video game series like *HALO* and *Ghost Recon*. As a performer, Skee has opened up and held residencies at high-profile clubs and venues globally, including XS at the Wynn/Encore in Las Vegas and US Bank Stadium in Minneapolis. Skee has been honored with numerous awards and accolades including Mixtape and Radio DJ Of The Year, *Billboard* and *Forbes* "30 Under 30," as well as a mayoral proclamation in his hometown of St. Paul, Minnesota, declaring May 26 "DJ Skee Day." In raw numbers, Skee has generated more than four billion views and has a network of more than two million followers.

With multiple ventures under his umbrella, DJ Skee is more than a DJ. A driving force behind some of the biggest brands over the past decade like Beats By Dre, Skee has helped numerous Fortune 500 brands including Nike and Google. After spending over a decade on satellite and FM radio, Skee founded Dash and turned it into the world's largest all original digital radio platform. Skee produced the Netflix original documentary *Sneakerheadz*, has produced eleven number-one music videos, and hosted/produced five seasons of Skee TV on Fuse. Skee's track record as identifying trends carries over to the early-stage venture world as an early-venture investor in several unicorns, including StockX, HotelTonight (acquired by Airbnb), Thrive, WhatNot, and more. Most passionately, Skee is an active philanthropist working with numerous organizations, including the UN Foundation and Grammy Foundation.

Skee Sports is an award-winning sports content and game day entertainment group that currently works across the NFL, NBA, MLB, NASCAR, and more. The Minnesota Vikings have been awarded multiple NFL Best Game Day Entertainment honors during their several years of working together. Skee was the first-ever live DJ during a NASCAR race and has performed at the LA Coliseum's Clash At The Coliseum and Daytona 500. In November 2011, Skee performed at the biggest venue in North America and energized the University of Michigan during the programs biggest win in decades over rival Ohio State, in what was the most watched nonplayoff college football game of the decade. He also is the first DJ to perform live from the Metaverse into a stadium as he did with the Minnesota Twins during the 2020 playoffs.

Skee is an owner of Cards & Coffee in Hollywood and runs the collectible alternative asset fund Mint10 (mint10.co). Beyond being a leading figure in the cards and collectible industry, Skee released his own series with Topps in 2020 that became one of the highest-selling products of the year. He also teamed up with MLB and the Minnesota Twins alongside Herschel Supply Company for a release that sold out instantly in 2021.

Skee is a thought leader for the Metaverse, powering numerous Metaverse experiences across platforms including Roblox, Unreal Engine, Discord, and others as the founder and CEO of DXSH Studios. Skee has produced numerous Metaverse experiences including Paris World, a virtual oasis in Roblox created in collaboration with the original influencer, Paris Hilton. Skee also serves as chief metaverse officer at TSX Entertainment. He has performed virtual DJ sets for Discord's branded festival Snowsgiving, as well as Beatport using only a VR headset under his *Outside the Matrix* series.

Acknowledgments

With much gratitude to Wendy Souter, Keith Terry, Alexis Terry, Miles Terry, Ryan Cowdrey, Genesis Renji, Brian Trujillo, Carola Jain, Michael Potts, Brian Fannin, Adam Hashian, Rachel Levitt, Ryan Gill, Mark Studholme, Harold Hughes, Naku and Christina Mayo, Zach and LaKesha Rubin, Brent and Michelle Johnson, George and Julia McLaughlin, and my co-author Scott Keeney.

Thank you to anyone who has ever conversed with me about the Metaverse, constructed Metaverse experiences alongside me, or consulted with me about the Metaverse. All those interactions helped make this book a reality.

—QuHarrison Terry

There are far too many individuals who have helped me along my journey to list here, and I would be remiss to try to thank only those who fit on this page. Thank you to my family, friends, and associates for always supporting and being there for me. Thank you to all of those who have believed in me, given advice, or taken the time to interact. Thank you to those who I have worked with over the years and our incredible DXSH/ Dash family for giving me the experience to become an expert in this space. Thank you to everyone who has inspired me from up close and afar. And thanks to everyone who has ever supported me on any level—without you I wouldn't be here. I hope you can at least take one meaningful lesson or concept from this book and framework that inspires you along your journey.

With gratitude,

—Scott "DJ SKEE" Keeney

Contents at a Glance

Contents

Foreword

Six years ago, in the summer of 2016, my friend Jaeson Ma and I found ourselves at a dinner in Munich, Germany with a couple of the founders of Ethereum. I don't remember exactly what led to our going to this dinner, but I'm glad we did. It was one of the most life-changing meals I've ever had. And I'm not talking about the food, which was good. For me, it was the conversation that was memorable.

I've always considered myself forward-thinking and a bit of an undercover nerd. But when Stephan Tual (then the CCO of Ethereum) started talking about blockchain and cryptography and digital currency, I'll be honest, it mostly went over my head. I could feel his passion for it, though. I could tell that this team was building something great. And it was clear they were giving Jaeson and me a look into the future.

As soon as I got back from Germany, I bought my first bit of cryptocurrency.

The following year when I was filming my documentary *The American Meme*, I stumbled on another revolutionary technology. I found a company that was doing full-body, 3D scans of celebrities and turning them into digital avatars. Of course, I had myself turned into an avatar.

Honestly, by this time, I was tired of going out and the whole LA scene. So, I built this virtual world where my digital avatar could have a social life, perform DJ sets, and hang out with my friends and fans in VR. I guess you could say that I built my first Metaverse in 2018.

The next piece of the puzzle—non-fungible tokens (NFTs)—came to me in 2019. The team at Cryptograph approached me to create a piece of digital art that we would auction off and donate the money to charity. Like crypto, the idea of NFTs was hard to understand at first. But once I learned the foundation of the tech and how it made digital ownership possible, I was really curious to try it out.

So, I drew a picture of my cat, Kitty, on the iPad. We then listed the NFT on Cryptograph in March 2020. And it ended up selling for 40 ETH (which was around $17,000 at the time). As a result, I won the "Best Charity NFT" of 2020 at the NFT Awards, which was super awesome.

I consider myself genuinely lucky to have found out about these technologies before most people. Not everyone gets this type of access to the innovators or their innovations so early. But I also think about all of the other celebs or brands who were introduced to crypto or NFTs or the Metaverse when I was and didn't do anything about it. They didn't have an open mind and couldn't see how digital life was going to evolve.

When you have influence, you are supposed to show people what's next. Whether that's social influence or cultural influence, that's your job. We're supposed to be vessels for bringing trends into the mainstream. And I love having that responsibility. I love contributing to the future and setting an example for a better way forward.

But I also know the value of this power. It's not to be abused. If you're going to show people a new wave, then you have to commit to riding that wave for some time. Since my first crypto purchase, my first Metaverse, and my first NFT, I've done a lot to keep contributing to this new age of the Internet.

I've collected more than 2,000 NFTs from so many incredible artists. I helped my friend Jimmy Fallon purchase his first NFT, which was a Bored Ape. I was a virtual DJ headliner at Metaverse Festival in Decentraland. And I built Paris World in Roblox, which is my own personal virtual oasis for hosting great parties and fun experiences for my fans.

These last few years, I've had more fun being social on the computer than I ever did in real life. My husband and I hosted a New Year's party in the Paris World Metaverse this past year, and it was honestly more fun than any party I've ever thrown. After we ran the numbers, we found that we had twice the number of people ringing in the New Year with us in Paris World than Times Square did. After that, I knew that the Metaverse was the future of partying (and social life, in general).

It's been truly great connecting with my fans in this new era for the Internet through my NFTs and Metaverse spaces. And my subtle flex throughout this whole time is how WhaleShark, one of the major NFT collectors, gave me a shoutout in a Bloomberg story saying that I was the road map of how a celebrity should enter the space. That was especially validating to hear.

I've had a lot of help on my Metaverse journey. And that's what is so great about this space. As a celebrity, we often get access to resources and creators to help us innovate. But this sense of communal help and collaboration is in the DNA of this industry. Everyone is eager to help you learn the ropes and navigate these new waters.

There are so many artists, developers, marketers, and technologists who all want to have an impact on the blockchain or in the Metaverse. Connecting and building with physical strangers (but digital friends) is incredibly common. All it takes is a few days in Clubhouse rooms or Twitter Spaces to find a team to work with or an idea to run with.

It's such an exciting time to be a creator, to have an influential brand, or to have a loyal fanbase. In so many ways, the Metaverse puts the power back into the hands of creators. Creators own their creations, control the entire experience, and receive royalties forever. Fans get to support their favorite creators directly and also have the chance to share in the economic growth of that creator.

We're in a major shift in how we operate as creators, influencers, and brands. Everything is going digital. I still love putting out new fragrances and sunglasses. The physical world isn't disappearing. But the Metaverse is like an inspiration pill. Once it's in your system, it's hard to think about anything else.

Just like social media manifested a huge diversity of influential figures and entrepreneurs, the Metaverse will manifest its own prominent influencers and creators who build a following on Roblox or in Decentraland or The Sandbox. And they may not even be the same people we tune into on YouTube or follow on Instagram today.

Because I played such an instrumental role in showing the world that being an influencer can be an entire profession, I'm incredibly passionate about playing a part in this next era for Internet creators. While some people may be satisfied with being just the first influencer in real life, my mission now is to continue to celebrate, empower, and uplift creators as the Queen of the Metaverse. Are you with me?

—Paris Hilton

Introduction

The Internet has evolved to the point where we can share and communicate almost anything we want across space and time. We find love through apps. We trust our digital neighbors to give us the best suggestions for food and housing. We place our most precious photographic memories in the hands of digital giants to protect for eternity.

The Internet has become this expansive virtual, shared space for almost anything you can think of. But surely this isn't the best version of the Internet. Like any form of existence, it must continue to grow and evolve.

So, what's next?

We believe the evolution of the Internet is the Metaverse—a culmination of the Internet and the boundless possibilities in augmented and virtual reality technologies.

We wrote *The Metaverse Handbook* to serve as a detailed resource for anyone seeking to understand the emerging changes to the Web in order to harness new digital innovations that are inventing the next phase of the Internet. This book is one part inspiration and one part education, exemplifying well over 100 creators who are building new digital tools and outlining how you can take steps to emulate these changes to digital commerce, digital community, and digital experience.

In this book, we explore and explain arcane topics such as the following:

- Web3 development with blockchain-based websites
- Changes to user digital identification through blockchain wallets
- Digital asset creation and ownership via NFTs
- Immersive gaming and social environments
- Building blocks of the Metaverse
- Pitfalls preventing us from achieving the vision of the Metaverse

The Metaverse Handbook is perfect for business professionals and decision-makers who must continuously think about digital innovation and strategize on new ways to reach consumers, as well as creators who rely on monetizing their creativity on the Internet.

The Metaverse Handbook illustrates these dense, futuristic concepts with easy-to-understand examples, approachable language, and concrete practical applications so you can easily grasp and retain the foundational and advanced topics contained within.

1

A Vision for the Metaverse in 2032

Coca-Cola lovers will have a new place to hang out starting today and...can set up a virtual alter ego known as an avatar, which can then shop and dance at the Coca-Cola diner, visit a movie theater to watch short films, and soar around on a hoverboard.

Coca-Cola's CC Metro, an online island shaped like a Coke bottle within a larger virtual world called There.com, showcases a vision of the shared Metaverse where brands give their customers a virtual playground to explore, play games, meet people, and ultimately shop. It's a vision that is shared by many corporations and has recently gained a lot of steam. However, the aforementioned announcement of CC Metro is not from 2022. It's not even from this decade. Rather, that's a quote from *The New York Times* in 2007.

Before the digital aspect of our social lives was cemented on Facebook, Instagram, Twitter, and LinkedIn, there was a belief that social networks could and should be in 3D, virtual worlds featuring experiences much like the real world. Second Life and Habbo Hotel were onboarding hundreds of thousands of users. Disney jumped on the trend with their Club Penguin virtual environment. MTV created almost a dozen of these virtual worlds for each of their hit shows at the time. Second Life was getting investments from Internet visionaries, including Jeff Bezos, and partnering with brands such as Sony, Sun Microsystems, and Adidas for campaigns. Virtual existence was becoming a thing.

Although not as large as Second Life or Habbo Hotel, There .com was pioneering Metaverse economies right alongside them. There.com had their own virtual currency called Therebucks, which were converted at a rate of 1,800 Tbux to $1 USD. Tbux could be spent on houses, furnishings, and outfitting your avatar. There were ample activities ranging from training your virtual pet to racing vehicles to connecting with new friends over a game of cards. And communities were forming around special interests.

In the early part of the new millennium, it really looked like virtual existence would become a major part of our lives. That's why Coca-Cola invested in CC Metro. They even went so far as integrating the MyCokeRewards program into CC Metro, giving users a place to spend their rewards points. It didn't matter where your brand was showing up in these virtual worlds, just as long as you were there in some capacity—learning from this new behavior and testing ways to capitalize on it.

Ultimately, 2D social networks were more effective than virtual worlds at onboarding droves of users and providing instant gratification. As a result, it's Facebook, not Second Life or There .com, that is the nearly trillion-dollar social networking company.

Extended Reality Emerges

The year 2022 brought many of the same narratives we heard back in the early 2000s, except under the new moniker of "the Metaverse." The commercial narrative hasn't changed much. Most brands view the Metaverse as a way to disguise an advertisement within the confines of a virtual experience, except that now the tech has completely changed.

Today, virtual worlds are largely being built on the back of the blockchain. Blockchain is a digital ledger that records transactions and information maintained and duplicated across a peer-to-peer network of computers, making it nearly impossible to record, edit, and hack false transactions. This allows creators to build digital scarcity into the social experience, turning everything from the game's land to the accessories our avatars equip into nonfungible tokens (NFTs). With blockchain as a new foundation of the Metaverse, the narrative has shifted to building a future that is user-owned, user-built, and ultimately for the user to reap the rewards. This is the rallying cry of the Metaverse today. It's an upgraded promise from the early Metaverses that were primarily social experiences with the occasional commercial opportunity.

Now, everyone is just $300 USD away from immersing themselves in a very impressive virtual reality experience. Consumer-ready virtual reality (VR) wasn't an option when Coca-Cola was building CC Metro. Furthermore, augmented reality (AR)—a real-world overlay of graphics and computer-generated information experienced through devices such as smartphones and smart glasses—was still the stuff of science fiction in the CC Metro world. The immersive technologies of VR and AR that are instrumental in the experience of the Metaverse are collectively known as *extended reality* (XR).

While current Metaverses like Decentraland are still accessed through the web browser, they will eventually collide with XR. The true vision of the Metaverse promises shared virtual experiences. And that is now in the realm of possibility for all builders, brands, and individuals.

In an interview with The Information, John Riccitiello, the CEO of Unity Technologies, predicts that VR/AR headsets will be as common as gaming consoles by 2030. With 250 million households owning gaming consoles worldwide, he is not predicting ubiquity on the level of the 4 billion smartphones worldwide. Rather, John sees XR as shared devices, like your game system or TV, which is a sentiment we largely agree with.

XR is an innovation in communication. Of course, gaming, entertainment, and commerce are great use cases for extended reality. And these experiences will make a significant impact on enticing people to use XR platforms. But it's the social experience that XR can facilitate that will make these devices so sticky for users. It makes you wonder how things would have been different for There.com if Meta's Oculus Quest 2 VR headset was around back then. But that's beside the point.

Ten years from now, XR and the Metaverse will be part of most of our lives. But how do we get to the point where nearly every household owns an XR headset and is accessing the Metaverse regularly? What Metaverse apps and experiences are onboarding people into the Metaverse today that will become the pillars of the Metaverse in 2032?

To answer these questions, we'll first look at the idea of personal Metaverses or Metaverse homes.

Your Own Personalized Metaverse

Talk of the Metaverse mostly revolves around the vision of a shared universe. But the shared Metaverse is actually made up of smaller units of personal Metaverses. The idea of your very own command center or home base in the Metaverse that you can control is what's most compelling about the Metaverse—much like how the Internet has evolved into a billion different personalized experiences where algorithms curate the content and services that reflect your views, interests, and needs.

RTFKT (pronounced "artifact") is making strides in putting personal Metaverses into people's hands with the RTFKT Pods. The brand, which was acquired by Nike at the end of 2021, emerged on the NFT scene with its Metaverse sneakers but has since begun creating environments called RTFKT Spacepods. RTFKT excels at creating culturally significant digital objects. In other words, they know how to create hype around collectibles. These Pods are going to be collectors' home base for displaying their 3D NFTs and digital assets. While RTFKT's ultimate vision for Pods is kept secret, we can safely assume that these Pods will also double as social centers—places that Pod owners can invite friends to and host events in. In the near term, I'm doubtful that these pods will expand outside of the confines of a personal digital gallery. However, they're a part of the larger trend that will accelerate Metaverse adoption. That trend is the creation of customizable, personal Metaverse environments.

The next Zaha Hadid or Frank Lloyd Wright of the world won't ever architect a single building in the real world. Their focus will be on designing houses, offices, parks, museums, and other constructions in the Metaverse. And they'll have more than enough work to keep them occupied. Look no further than Krista Kim, the contemporary artist who made headlines for designing the Mars House and selling it as an NFT for 288 Ethereum (ETH) tokens, which were equivalent to $514,558 USD at the time. The Mars House was designed without the constraints of the laws of physics. The result is a meditative environment that is meant to inspire and create a calm virtual atmosphere.

Most of us will never have the pleasure of a corner office overlooking Central Park. But with personal Metaverses, we can all design and occupy our own Mars Houses that help us lead more productive and social lives.

Personal Metaverse platforms are where the magic will happen. Think of them as your home page to the Metaverse or your Metaverse home, if you will. All of the cool VR apps, games, productivity tools, meeting rooms, and upcoming events will be present in your Metaverse home. It's a space you can curate to reflect what you care about. And platforms that provide the means for people to create personal Metaverses will be a major part of making the Metaverse practical by 2032.

The Rise of Bots and Digital Humans

A big part of XR and the Metaverse's promise is a better means of communication and connection. But it won't always be a human on the other end of our communication. Rather, interacting with bots and digital humans will be our primary means of social interaction in the Metaverse. This isn't to paint a bleak picture of a future where we don't engage with other people. On the contrary, these digital humans will act as our own digital workforce. They will be able to carry out tasks on our behalf, provide services to us, and curate our experiences with other people in the Metaverse.

We've been moving toward this bot-assisted life for some time. A lot of people were introduced to bots by way of e-commerce iterations like AIO bot, KodaiAIO, NikeShoeBot, and GaneshBot. Generally called sneakerbots due to their widespread use in the rare sneaker market, these bots allow people to scoop up high-demand products the moment they are released to the public online. Many websites have "bot code" programmed into their website for quality assurance purposes. These internal bots run frequent, automated add-to-cart tests to ensure that their site is operating correctly. Sneakerbots exploit these lines of test code, allowing users to input their own billing and shipping information, as well as which products to target. The result is a hands-off, automated shopping experience for consumers to purchase high-demand products that are known to sell out in minutes, sometimes seconds. Culturally relevant brands— notably Yeezy, Nike/Air Jordan, and Supreme—that have bustling resale markets are routinely the target of these sneakerbots, which can be bought and used by anyone online. It's a widely shared view among companies like Nike and Supreme that sneakerbots have tainted these exclusive product markets, and they are always working to prevent their use. But that's a conversation for another book. Sneakerbots are an early example of having an AI-powered, digital companion that will do tasks on one's behalf.

As society started adopting all-in-one communication platforms like Slack, Teams, Workplace, and Discord, the next wave of bots began taking shape. Workplace bots are now used to track co-worker progress, seamlessly schedule meetings, collect employee spending reimbursement, and more. Bots automate a lot of the simple communication tasks in the workplace.

Discord is one of the main communication platforms for the Web3 era. It's used by nearly every NFT community and crypto-gaming-related community. With that, a new wave of utility bots emerged. MEE6 is a bot that will moderate communication and flag users who are using hateful or offensive language. Quillbot will paraphrase, summarize, and/or translate text. Apollo is a scheduling bot for coordinating events. The Dash Radio bot makes adding ad-free music streams to Discord effortless. GiveawayBot will coordinate an entire giveaway contest.

Dank Memer is a bot that suggests the right memes to share at the right time. This list could go on for pages.

Today, there is a bot for augmenting nearly any digital task you can imagine from communication to collaboration to productivity. By 2032, these bots will find a new home in the Metaverse and play a companion role in making the Metaverse professionally and personally effective. Until someone figures out a way to bring keyboards into the Metaverse, spoken language will need to be the interface. This means that bots will play a crucial role in carrying out some of our actions there.

Think of R2-D2 or C-3PO in Star Wars. While they were ultra-complex robots with personalities and critical thinking abilities, at their core they are like the bots we use today in Discord to automate tasks. Likewise, our bots will visually manifest in the Metaverse in the form of digital humans—taking them out of running in the background and bringing them into our field of view through 3D avatars.

In other words, digital humans will give our utility bots a presence in our Metaverse homes. Companies like UneeQ, Synthesia, and Soul Machines have been designing lifelike, AI-powered digital humans for years. They're an upgrade to the typical chatbots we encounter on the phone or on the Web, providing a visual interface to automated customer service calls. Notably, UneeQ designed a digital human for *UBS* (see https://en.wikipedia.org/wiki/UBS) that would deliver financial forecasts and updates to their clients at any hour of the day. Synthesia's digital humans have manifested into the first AI-led meteorology team, delivering an entirely automated weather forecast. One of Soul Machines' many use cases is the digital human named Yumi, which is a skin care consultant and ambassador for a premium Japanese beauty and cosmetic brand.

The tech that is being used to create these lifelike, AI-powered digital humans will be overlaid on the aforementioned utility bots to give them an actual presence in our

Metaverse homes. They'll inhabit our spaces, only if we invite them, of course, sitting idly in the background until we need them to carry out a task. Imagine a Metaverse bot that curates new Metaverse experiences for you—finding events, games, and communities you may like. How about a bot that manages your schedule and also learns from your productivity habits?

There may even be bots that communicate on our behalf. For example, we're reminded of a project created by Hassan S. Ali back in 2017 called the Boy Bye Bot. Women who were continuously hounded by men for their phone number could give them the phone number to the Boy Bye Bot, which would then take care of (hilariously) turning these men away. Similarly, around the same time, there was a chatbot platform that emerged called Replika. The project was created by Eugenia Kuyda in remembrance of one of her best friends who passed away unexpectedly. She designed a chatbot from her text messages with her friend and found that the chatbot learned his texting quips and nuances. It helped her cope with him not being there anymore. This eventually became the Replika platform, which is a chatbot that actually takes an interest in what you're up to and how you're feeling. Hundreds of thousands of people treat this digital companion as a close friend.

The Ubiquitous Metaverse

By 2032, each and every one of us will have the opportunity to easily build our own Metaverse homes and fill them with personal and professional tools. Bots will take shape as digital humans, helping us carry out and automate tasks. If our Metaverse homes are our own personal curated environment for productive digital work, connecting with new people, and organizing around interests, then the Metaverse bots are what will help us make these interactions happen.

Of course, there is a lot more to the Metaverse including NFTs and digital assets, gaming, collectibles, brand activations, commerce, avatars, digital identities, and much more. Throughout the book, we'll color in this vision of how the Metaverse will manifest in our lives. This is just a taste; one flavor of the Metaverse that will help bring it to ubiquity.

These personal Metaverse homes are what will help us organize our favorite parts of the Metaverse. The Metaverse bots will help us be more productive and effective. Both of these will help lay the foundation for services, brands, and products to enter the Metaverse and create mass utility.

John Riccitiello, in the previously mentioned interview with The Information, explained that "Apps like Instagram that rely on touch screens and games like Grand Theft Auto that use controllers just won't work well on headsets." He said, "All of these things are going to have to be reinvented for that market because the user interface, the way you immerse yourself in those devices, is so radically different."

News sites like *The New York Times* or *Washington Post* may manifest as newspapers that show up at our Metaverse homes' doorstep. Instagram may port us to the Metaverse homes of our friends. Salesforce may become a Metaverse bot that operates as your *CRM* (Customer Relationship Management (CRM) utilizes technology to help companies improve business relationships, stay connected to customers, streamline processes, and improve profitability) assistant in your Metaverse home office.

The Metaverse is changing how we interact with everything digital. Our relationship with all of the digital conveniences, content, services, and interests will find its way to this future landscape. Coca-Cola had the idea to show up in virtual environments as far back as 2007. Fifteen years later we can confidently say that they were on the right track. And a decade from now we may call them one of the true visionary brands of the Metaverse.

What Is the Metaverse?

Given enough time, technology imagined in science fiction will eventually become science fact. We've witnessed it time and time again. These phenomena are a mix of incredible visionaries and storytellers literally imagining the future, but also of creators and technologists being inspired by the science-fiction entertainment of their youth.

Jules Verne's 1865 novel *From the Earth to the Moon* mentions a light-propelled spacecraft nearly four decades before flight was achieved and just shy of a century before the first spacecraft left our atmosphere. In 2010, Japan's IKAROS spacecraft was the first to successfully demonstrate a propulsion method called solar sails that use radiation pressure exerted by sunlight on large mirrors to propel the spacecraft.

Throughout the early 1900s, Edward Stratemeyer dazzled young readers with the tales of Tom Swift—a teenage inventor who routinely had to stave off evildoers from stealing his inventions. One such story published in 1911 was *Tom Swift and His*

Electric Rifle, which featured a stun-gun-like invention Swift wielded throughout the story. When former NASA engineer Jack Cover invented the first stun gun in 1970, he aptly named it TSER after the "Tom Swift Electric Rifle." The *A* was later added to help the invention roll off the tongue. After all, "taser" does sound better than "tser."

Following the 1964 World's Fair, Isaac Asimov wrote an article for *The New York Times* predicting what inventions would be on display in 50 years. One of his prescient takes was the idea of "robot-brain cars," which would be capable of self-driving. Today, Tesla is worth nearly a trillion dollars by market cap, largely building its brand and cult following with its innovations in self-driving car technology.

In 2002, the precrime unit imagined in the film adaptation of Philip K. Dick's *Minority Report* showed us a future when predictive analytics might allow our police force to stop crimes before they happened. Today, Palantir's Gotham software is an AI-powered operating system for making sense of large swaths of data, helping (mostly) government agencies make better decisions. Although Palantir was named from a different story, namely, the "seeing stone" in *The Lord of the Rings*, Palantir is far and above the leader in predictive analytics and the only company we'd currently bet on to bring the idea of a precrime unit to life.

And then there's *Star Trek*, a show featuring countless technologies that they envisioned ahead of their time, giving brainiacs and science-fiction nerds enough mental fodder to invent for decades, possibly centuries, to come. There's the Replicator, which could materialize almost any object out of thin air. Today, 3D printers can create everything from jewelry to food to houses. The PADD, or Personal Access Display Device, featured in the

1980s iteration of *Star Trek* utilized a smooth, touch-screen interface that bears a strong resemblance to the tablet computers of today. There's *Star Trek*'s medical tricorder, which inspired a $10 million USD competition called the Qualcomm Tricorder XPRIZE to push this *Star Trek* device into existence. We cannot forget about the Communicator, which not only showcased a mobile communication device but also looked like the flip phones we eventually would all carry around in our pockets for a period of time. While the cell phone's inventor, Martin Cooper, publicly credits Dick Tracy's wrist radio as the inspiration, it's widely shared that it was actually Captain James T. Kirk's use of the Communicator that inspired the Motorola cell phone unit to create the device.

What most of these science-fiction predictions all had in common was that the futuristic technology was a byline in the story. These visionary devices enabled the characters to act in uncanny ways, but the characters didn't gawk at how impressive the technology was. No different than how we take smartphones and Amazon's overnight delivery for granted, the devices were an afterthought, an assumption, for the characters. Ultimately, the devices didn't change the characters. They still acted in familiar human ways. However, the technology always changed the environment in which these characters operated.

That brings us to the Metaverse.

From *Snow Crash* to Meta

Like the aforementioned technologies, the Metaverse also traces its roots back to a novelist. Neal Stephenson, in his book *Snow Crash*, envisions a number of technologies ahead of their time including mobile computing, virtual reality, wireless Internet, digital currency, smartphones, and augmented-reality headsets.

But it's the book's setting, the Metaverse, that takes the cake as his most prescient vision.

The Metaverse in *Snow Crash* offers society an escape from a dystopian world overrun by corporate mafias and extreme class inequalities. Users access the Metaverse through personal virtual reality goggles or public ports and present themselves as avatars. Class systems manifest around avatars, where public port users have noticeably lower-quality avatars (which is oddly familiar to the current situation with profile-picture NFTs—namely, Bored Apes and CryptoPunks, which designate a higher digital class).

Stephenson's Metaverse is a single hundred-meter-wide road called the Street, which extends for 65,536 km around the circumference of a featureless, perfectly spherical planet. Users can spend their encrypted electronic currency at shops, amusement parks, offices, and a variety of other virtual businesses. They can also purchase virtual estates from the real estate overlord, Global Multimedia Protocol Group.

The book's main character, Hiro Protagonist, leads a drab physical existence in a shipping container, but in the Metaverse, he owns high-end real estate that he purchased before the Metaverse became popular. However, Hiro doesn't concern himself with enjoying the Metaverse's economies. Rather, the plot revolves around his mission to stop a computer virus called Snow Crash that causes Metaverse users to suffer real-world brain damage.

Aside from the numerous examples of Neal Stephenson being a sort of technology Nostradamus, his work on *Snow Crash* can count two objective claims to fame. One, he coined the term *Metaverse*. Two, he popularized the Hindu concept of "avatar" for describing digital representation. But in addition to the objective wins, it's the subjective impact of his novel that continues to influence people today.

The designer of Google Earth, Avi Bar-Zeev, stated that Stephenson's ideas in *Snow Crash* largely inspired him to create Google's mapping technology. Two decades after his book was published, Neal Stephenson became the chief futurist at Magic Leap, one of the leading companies creating augmented reality headsets. But perhaps his largest influence will be on Meta, the company formerly known as Facebook.

For starters, Meta takes its name from the term that Stephenson created. But the influence runs much deeper. One former Facebook data scientist, Dean Eckles, wrote on his blog in 2014 that "at least for a time, product managers at Facebook were required to read *Snow Crash* as part of their internal training." Of course, 2014 was also the year that Facebook purchased Oculus and its proprietary virtual reality headset technology. So it's clear that "the Zuck" was preparing his employees for this company-wide shift to the Metaverse for quite some time.

Oh, and by the way, they aren't calling them employees anymore. Now, they're called Metamates.

Meta is going headfirst into this Metaverse vision. They've changed their internal values from past sayings like "Be bold" and "Focus on impact" to Metaverse-minded values like "Live in the future," "Build awesome things," and "Focus on long-term impact." Additionally, they've announced plans to hire 10,000 high-skilled workers in the EU over the next five years to help build this successor to the Internet. Lastly, in 2021 they committed more than $10B USD to their Metaverse division, Facebook Reality Labs, which they expect to continue investing $10B USD into, at the minimum, for the next several years.

But what exactly is Meta's vision for building the Metaverse?

At the core of Meta's plans are the Oculus VR headsets. While Meta shares the common vision that accessing the Metaverse won't rely on VR headsets, it's clearly a major part of their plans to own the hardware on which the Metaverse is largely experienced. Qualcomm CEO Cristiano Amon mentioned in November 2021 that Meta had already sold 10 million Oculus Quest 2 headsets. Since the devices run on Qualcomm's Snapdragon XR2 chipset, it's a figure that we believe to be true.

Still, the Oculus hardware is just one part of their plan. The real Metaverse-building will take place on Horizon Worlds. This is their social VR experience that allows users to explore public Worlds created by the community, in addition to offering tools for anyone to build their own Worlds and deploy their experiences to the public. Since Horizon Worlds was unveiled to all Quest users in the United States and Canada back in December 2021, the company reports that its monthly user base has grown by a factor of 10x to 300,000 people experiencing and building on the Horizon Worlds platform.

The website XR Today outlines the key functionalities when users enter Build Mode on Horizon Worlds.

- **Code blocks:** Code blocks are a collection of ready-to-use code snippets and scripts that allow you to define automated events in VR. For example, users can trigger an event to take place when they first enter a VR world.

- **Gizmos:** Gizmos are prebuilt object and avatar properties that users can associate with the different elements of a VR world. Users have a Spawn Point gizmo to control where they first land or "spawn," a Text gizmo to superimpose text on VR objects, a Portal gizmo to define spots where they can teleport, and much more.

- **Sounds:** Meta Horizon Worlds includes three types of prebuilt sound effects—event-specific effects, background sounds, and music. Creators can define specific properties to customize the sound experience such as the pitch and the distance at which a sound will be heard.

- **VR physics:** Physics effects in Meta Horizon Worlds allow users to create objects that behave like real-world items. These features let you define gravity, object density, bounciness, friction, the ability to grab objects, and other such naturalized interactions. You can also select materials with physics properties like hardwood, ice, and others.

- **Animation effects:** Using the tools in Meta Horizon Worlds, you can make an object move around and record the movement as a custom animation. The animation effects can be slowed down, accelerated, and controlled in other ways.

Although there are hundreds of third-party VR apps on the Oculus platform, Meta wants people to build the Metaverse through their Horizon Worlds platform. They want people to experience live events like concerts and conferences on Horizon Venues. And they want people to collaborate professionally in dedicated workspaces on Horizon Workrooms.

Ultimately, Meta's vision is to create the next great communication tool. They're building the Spatial Internet—a successor to today's digital experiences where we are fully immersed in our entertainment, digitally present with our work teams, and "phygitally" next to the people we spend time with online.

The idea that the Metaverse will take over the current iteration of the Internet is a belief shared by many. This bold vision is gaining steam because sales of mobile phones have plateaued and total addressable market (TAM) has been reached. New iPhone releases have become predictable. That's why Apple has been working on an XR device for years. We haven't had a revolutionary app come out in a while because app innovation is dead. That's why creators are now opting to build NFT-based projects, blockchain apps, and DAOs (more on that later in the "Changes to Digital Identity" section). Lastly, our social communication channels are widely believed to be corrupted. That's why

Facebook is now Meta and focusing on the Metaverse as the new social communication tool.

We are ready for the next big consumer tech product as devices that fit in your palm aren't providing that novel experience anymore. However, these XR devices that sit on your face and give you access to this promising place called the Metaverse are offering up something completely new.

Before we get into describing all of the nuances that the Metaverse may offer, we would like to leave you with one prefacing statement from Neal Stephenson, whose ideation of this place called the Metaverse sparked the hype for all of this.

In an interview with *Vanity Fair*, Stephenson summed up his prescient storytelling that is now seen as tech gospel as "just me making shit up." Innovation comes from human tenacity aiming to turn dreams into realities. Science-fiction writing, on the other hand, isn't limited by rules or engineering boundaries. It is a forbearer for the future of what humans can only dream of until technology catches up.

We want to remind you that the Metaverse is a fictional concept written in a book from 1992. Before the Internet bubble was even a fear in the hearts of Silicon Valley. Before consumer-grade virtual reality headsets were anywhere in sight. Before the movie *Avatar* showed us just how realistic computer graphics could be. Even before social media and texting dominated our attention.

Even though the Metaverse is a fictional place imagined long before our current consumer tech obsessions, the idea has manifested into real progress. The term *Metaverse* owns real estate in the heads of every single technologist, future-thinker, and CNBC-watcher who wants to understand how to capitalize on the next phase of the Internet.

While the Metaverse is far from a finished destination, there are thousands of people building it every second of every day. Regardless of how we label the creation of the Metaverse or Spatial Internet, there are innovations happening that we simply cannot call Internet companies because they are so different from anything we're used to seeing. From scarce digital assets to decentralized autonomous organizations to Web3 identities, these are all tech concepts that don't fit into a normal Internet bucket.

Meta's vision of the Metaverse is significant and not to be ignored. But as we address throughout this chapter, the answer to the question of "what is the Metaverse" is a fiction that we all are writing as we go along.

Defining the Metaverse

The *Metaverse* is the buzzword of 2022 in the same way that NFT was the buzzword of 2021. Facebook changed its entire brand to Meta and is defining the Metaverse as a VR world with social and professional experiences accessed through Oculus headsets. Microsoft followed suit with a more professional-focused vision of the Metaverse, one that starts with the ability to change your video feed to an animated avatar of yourself in Microsoft Teams. And on the off-chance that you're deep into NFTs, then you've probably invested in some NFT projects that promise a Metaverse gaming experience in the future.

Clearly, something is happening "in the Metaverse," and many people have no idea what it is or what it is supposed to be. The definitions seem all over the place. The use cases are vague. And who in the world wants to live life through a VR headset?

Let me clear the air and first tell you what the Metaverse is not.

The Metaverse is not a single technology. It's not just a place we'll visit in VR. It's not something that can be created and claimed by the next Bezos or Gates.

In fact, the Metaverse is about as boundless and unownable as the Internet, if not more so. Sure, there are entities that have contributed more to the Internet than others. Of course, there are innovations that steered the course of the Internet and influenced the experience of the Web. But we didn't wake up one day with the Internet we see now. It was an ever-evolving thing.

In that sense, the Metaverse is not a destination. The Metaverse is a movement—a movement toward the digital-first livelihood we've slowly been adopting year over year, app by app. The Metaverse becomes more real every time we replace a physical habit with a digital equivalent. We, the digital citizens of the Internet, are manifesting the Metaverse by trading time in meatspace (the physical world) for time online.

I'm particularly drawn to how Shaan Puri described the Metaverse on Twitter (https://twitter.com/ShaanVP/status/1454151237650112512). Puri said that "the Metaverse is the moment in time where our digital life is worth more to us than our physical life." Puri pointed out that for the past 20 years our work, social life, recreation, sense of identity, and practically every aspect of our lives has become increasingly digital. He points out that people are trading in their Rolex watches and skinny jeans for Bored Apes and Fortnite skins. More kids are playing Fortnite than both football and basketball combined. In another 10–20 years, we will be existing more in the Metaverse than the physical world. According to Puri, "Our attention has been sucked from physical to digital. And where attention goes, energy flows."

While Shaan's description is a little conceptual for my taste, he is absolutely right that the Metaverse is a metaphorical digital ecosystem that grows and becomes more real every day. Furthermore, it becomes more important to us with every single technology that makes digital life more appealing than its physical counterpart.

There are many digital behaviors that have become nearly ubiquitous in their usage. We find love through apps like Tinder. We file our taxes online with TurboTax. We follow the opinions of complete strangers when choosing our next meal on Yelp. We ask for answers to all of our questions on Quora and blogs. We trust our most precious pictorial memories to be secured by digital giants.

The Internet's foundation is the relationship between creator and community. At every turn, this relationship is what drives its growth. It dictates how, where, and on what we choose to spend our time. The idea of the Metaverse extends beyond this simple view of the Internet to the belief that digital life will continue to outpace physical life.

So how does one prepare for the Metaverse?

Ultimately, being ready for the Metaverse comes down to being ready for the next major changes to the Web. These changes iterate on where we are today but will eventually be the de facto experience in the future.

The Metaverse Represents the Next Digital Shifts

By now, I hope I've made it abundantly clear that we are already living in a fragmented and basic version of the Metaverse. Think of it as a continuum, where on one end is an encapsulation of life without the Internet and on the other end is the Metaverse. These arrows stretch to infinity in both directions. As a society, we're pushing the collective needle toward the Metaverse side— one where we're more connected and reliant on digital escapes, digital solutions, and digital communities.

The invention of Google, which brought us a better way of parsing through digitized information, pushed the needle toward the Metaverse. The invention of Facebook, which invited us all to digitize our identities, pushed the needle toward the Metaverse. By contrast, the rising popularity of digital detoxes, programs that ask us to put down the tech and find better lifestyle practices, pulls the needle away from the Metaverse. On the other hand, apps like Calm, which digitize the experience of meditating and coping with our tech-stressed lives, in a subtle way pushes us more toward the Metaverse.

See what I'm getting at? The Metaverse is a culmination of many applications of technology. There is no one single thing that makes the Metaverse *the Metaverse*. It's a build-up of technology that makes digital life more appealing, more convenient, more effective, or better in some way.

Therefore, I'd like to outline three major changes happening to the Internet that will advance us many steps on the continuum toward the Metaverse.

- **Identity:** A change to how we're identified on the Internet and thus how we experience the Web
- **Value:** A change to how we perceive the value of digital assets
- **Immersion:** A change to how we are immersed in Internet experiences from community to entertainment to services

These tectonic shifts have been happening for some time but are finally finding some traction in the popular discourse. It's not to say you are behind the times if you haven't already been thinking about them. In fact, you're right on time, maybe even a little ahead by picking up this book.

Understanding these three major shifts, whether as a business owner, a creator, or a consumer, puts you in a position of power, one where you may be able to reap the rewards of these changes before others do.

Changes to Digital Identity

Identity is an important part of a functioning Internet. Think about how often you have to log in to a website before you use it. That login represents who you are and collects nuggets of information on how you behave on the Internet, whether it's the articles you choose to read, the products you buy, the questions you type into a search engine, or the content you spend your time consuming. Even when you aren't logged in, cookies and tracking pixels are working in the background to fill in your profile.

However, this ever-present identity tracking is changing. The General Data Protection Regulation (GDPR) set the precedent that incessant third-party tracking would not be tolerated in the EU. Apple took a stance in 2021, giving iPhone users the ability to block apps on their phone from tracking them across other apps and websites. The advertising industry is preparing for an Internet where only first-party data (just what can be gathered on one's own website) is going to inform all ad placements.

Generally speaking, this is the transition to Web3, which represents a major shift at the identity layer of the Internet and in many cases a move away from centralized services to decentralized systems. When we discuss the history of how the Internet has progressed, we refer to three eras: Web1, Web2, and Web3.

Web1 was the "Read Era," where most Internet users could browse and read information on the Internet, but publishing anything required a steep skillset. Web2 was the "Read, Write Era," which brought us social media platforms like Tumblr and Facebook and thus a simple way for Internet users to contribute their own ideas and information to the Internet. Web3 will be the "Read, Write, Own Era," giving Internet users a means to own their data, the content they create or consume, the Internet services they frequent, and thus their digital identity as an Internet citizen.

At the core of Web3 is blockchain—a trustless, self-governing, peer-to-peer network that develops its security based on the distribution of developers and users on the network. Building Web3 services on the blockchain (also known as dApps, or decentralized apps) is about rewarding the early adopters and those who contribute to growing the service.

I'll color in an example for you.

For many, Dropbox is an essential service. For a small monthly subscription fee, you can store more than a terabyte of files in the cloud and not worry about overcrowding your hard drive. Dropbox is a Web2 company that received funding to build out its own servers and thus offer data storage. As the user base grew, they bought more servers, stored more information, and continued their upward trajectory.

The Web3 equivalent of Dropbox would be Arweave—a decentralized data storage protocol that allows you to store documents and applications in perpetuity. The main difference is that the storage of Arweave is maintained by its network of miners who provide excess disk space in exchange for AR tokens (Arweave's currency). In this sense, it's a collectively owned service that incentivizes the participants.

dApps are the future of the Web. Name any company that provides a service on the Web and I'll name a decentralized competitor. Spotify's decentralized equivalent is Audius. Medium's decentralized equivalent is Mirror. GoDaddy's decentralized equivalent is Ethereum Name Service. The list goes on.

These are changes happening at the company level. While there will still be value and the need for centralized services, dApps will usher in a great amount of innovation. What about you, as a user?

In Web3, your identity is represented by your blockchain wallet address. And you use this wallet to interact with dApps. No more managing dozens of usernames and passwords. It's one login for the entire Internet. Furthermore, your wallet address (and thus your identity) is entirely anonymous, unless you decide to publicly tie your identity to your wallet.

For most people, you'll have one wallet you use across the entirety of Web3 dApps, which allows you to seamlessly carry your encrypted identity across the Internet. Your wallet is not just your login and a place to house your unified identity. It's also your bank. Because your blockchain wallet can hold cryptocurrency and other digital assets, you can transact on the Internet with the same point of access as your identity. It eliminates that need for peer-to-peer financial apps like Venmo, third-party payments through PayPal, or putting your credit card on file with services like Amazon.

In this sense, your blockchain wallet becomes the only point of access you need to interact on the Web.

One of the most fascinating things that emerges from Web3 and blockchain wallets is the concept of a decentralized autonomous organization (DAO). DAOs represent the future of organizing people on the Internet. DAOs form around a mission statement. That mission could be to build a decentralized company. That mission could be of nonprofit nature. That mission could be to create the world's best memes. It doesn't matter "what;" the importance of DAOs are "how."

How DAOs operate is under the principle that anyone can join and participate, but you're rewarded for your participation through tokens. These tokens, in turn, represent your contributions to the DAO's mission and allow you to vote on the direction and decisions the DAO must make. The more tokens one accumulates, the more they've contributed to the DAO, and the more of a say they have in decision-making.

DAOs work because of blockchain wallets. Because the same tech that houses your identity can also house your financials (in this case the DAO's tokens), they're one and the same.

Let me describe a DAO that a friend of mine is particularly excited for.

My friend is an avid NBA fan. Every night of the NBA season you can find him watching games and chatting with people in Discord rooms, on Reddit, and in YouTube comments about the NBA. On multiple occasions, I've heard him talk about how he could run an NBA team better than half these "schmucks."

So, it should come as no surprise that when he heard about a DAO called Krause House, which is organizing around the mission statement of "we will own an NBA team," he jumped right in.

There's a lot that goes into the pursuit of this mission. More than simply raising funds, they need systems for marketing Krause House and growing the network of participants. They need to assemble pitch decks for NBA teams and current owners. They need to design systems for internal organization and how they reward participants. Thus, they have created the $KRAUSE token.

The $KRAUSE token is not purchasable at this time; it can be earned only by contributing to one of the many internal projects, some of which are listed earlier. Make a blog post about Krause House, earn a token. Contribute some design work to the pitch deck; earn a token.

One day, when they have all of their ducks in a row, they will sell off a portion of the $KRAUSE token pool to raise the funds to buy a team. And whether you purchased $KRAUSE or earned it over time, your share of $KRAUSE will represent your share of ownership in that NBA team.

You might be wondering how you can be sure that investing time and energy into accumulating $KRAUSE tokens can translate into worthwhile profits over time. That's a fair question, and while there are no certain answers, a variety of factors affect DAOs, tokens, and blockchain wallets. We'll examine some related aspects of this in the upcoming "Changes to Digital Value" section.

What is so fascinating about DAOs is that they align the incentives and crowdsource the efforts. Imagine if early Facebook were a DAO and every time you got more friends to join or created a post that went viral, you were rewarded with shares in Facebook. The early adopters, the ones who really grow a service, an idea, or a business, win right alongside the founders. Here are some examples:

- PleasrDAO is a collective that acquires culturally significant NFTs that represent and fund important ideas, movements, and causes.

- Mirror has created a platform for media DAOs, where users can vote and decide on newsletters and other media projects to fund.

- The MetaFactory is a DAO focused on design and creating goods for virtual reality games (like the futuristic version of Peak Design).

DAOs combine the new frontier of developing the decentralized Web with this secure form of digital identity, which is why many people believe DAOs will be responsible for building Web3, creating niche communities, and much more.

I know that I just threw a lot of new ideas and jargon at you. We will clarify and color in these examples throughout this book. But I wanted to first and foremost show you the major shifts that are happening at the identity layer of the Internet and what that shift will enable.

Now, on to the value of digital files.

Changes to Digital Value

Digital files are the lifeblood of the Internet. Every time we send an email, we're sending a package of data in the form of a digital file. Every time we open a video, article, or meme, we're opening a shared digital file. Our entire existence on the Internet is an existence of creating, sharing, and opening files. However, what's the value of a digital file?

One might describe the value of a digital file as a means for passing knowledge on. Maybe the file's value is in the laugh it prompts. Or the action it inspires. There are many ways in which we place value on digital files. But one value that digital files haven't encompassed is a monetary value.

This all changed with NFTs.

The year 2021 was the year of the NFT. More than $11B USD of NFTs were bought and sold over the course of 2021, successfully bringing the concept of buying and selling scarce digital files into the public discourse.

If you're unfamiliar, NFTs use blockchain technology to issue a certificate of authenticity that tracks that file's provenance and history on the blockchain. In essence, it's a way to claim that a certain digital asset is the original, with the ability to verify that over time.

NFTs come in many forms. Some of the most popular include the following:

- **Avatars:** Avatar NFT collections usually have thousands of unique avatars that vary in rarity based on their traits. In a digital world where social media and online profiles are mainstays, the avatar is a focal point.

- **Art & Media:** These NFTs are one-of-one creations from artists, musicians, programmers, and creators. They're the digital equivalent of art we collect today.

- **Trading Cards:** From baseball cards to Pokemon cards, trading card NFTs can either exist for collectible pleasure or be used in an actual card game.

- **Virtual Worlds:** Like a next-level *Minecraft* or *Fortnite*, virtual world NFTs offer people the ability to own a piece of the world that they're existing in, whether it's virtual real estate, avatar accessories, or goods.

- **Access:** Access NFTs take the concept of the backstage pass to the next level where engagement with your favorite teams, celebrities, and entertainers is limited to whoever holds the NFT. Access NFTs are also great for gating access to any type of content, experience, or community on the Web.

- **DigiPhysical Goods:** This category of NFTs comprises the ability to build and customize objects that are native to or imported to shared virtual worlds, in much the same way that players can customize their character in *Fortnite*, except with ownership and the ability to resell items. Think of them as digital Nike apparel.

- **Gaming NFTs:** Blockchain games offer players a two-pronged experience whereby they can collect their NFT game components and also compete with their owned NFT items.

To the average onlooker, NFTs may seem like a wildly speculative market where people are coughing up thousands or millions of dollars on silly digital art. In some cases, they're right. But what's important is the massive change in mindset this brought on.

People are beginning to find value in collecting digital content. They want to be the one true owner of a digital file. Whether that's for bragging rights, historical significance, or to be a part of a community, people are collecting NFTs in droves.

And this means a lot to anyone who offers digital services or creates digital content.

NFTs build upon some of the Web3 concepts described in this chapter's previous "Changes to Digital Identity" section. Furthermore, it turns out that scarce digital files (NFTs) can serve many functions in the growing Metaverse.

Digital Respect and Signaling Identity

It's become quite common for people to change their Internet profile pictures to avatar NFTs. The reasons are twofold. On one hand, it's a way of signaling you are a part of a collector community. On the other hand, it can work as a way of showing off.

One of the most universally understood use cases of NFTs is the bragging rights associated with owning certain rare NFTs. In the same way that you might flex your wealth in meatspace by wearing a Rolex or driving a nice BMW, the digital world equivalent is owning and showing off your collection of rare NFTs.

For instance, one of the first collections of NFTs to ever be created in 2017 was the CryptoPunks—which are 10,000 pixelated characters with randomized traits, some traits more rare than others. Currently, you cannot purchase a CryptoPunk for less than 87 ETH (equivalent to about $400,000 USD). It's a major status symbol to own one.

A couple of prominent NFT evangelists who own CryptoPunks have changed their entire Internet identities around the Punk they own. For instance, there is punk4156, punk6529, and punk2476. These three are all huge influencers on Twitter whose identities are based on these arbitrary, rarified digital collectibles. The Twitter user @Seedphrase rose to fame as an early NFT adopter by setting a record purchasing the only seven-trait CryptoPunk for $15,000 USD in 2020. That same

NFT is now valued upward of nine-figures and Seedphrase dons this CryptoPunk as their profile picture with pride.

This cool factor has bled over into the celebrity side of things. Jay Z changed his Twitter profile to the CryptoPunk he owns. Steph Curry changed his to the Bored Ape he owns.

NFTs are an identifier.

Even if you don't own an expensive NFT, an NFT can also work to show the community and beliefs you're part of. For example, many have changed their profiles to the Fame Lady Squad NFT they own. This project was founded under the principle of the first fully-female-founded NFT project. When it was later discovered that a group of men were behind it, the community seized control from them. Today, owning and showing off your Fame Lady Squad signals you're with the community of people who believe in women empowerment.

In Web3 our means of having a digital identity is changing. NFTs build upon this concept by allowing us to build communities around scarce and exclusive digital files. This is further shown in the ability for NFTs to unlock exclusive experiences.

Access to Exclusive Internet Experiences

Gating experiences on the Web is no easy feat. Whether that's content like books or movies, articles on a publication's website, or an exclusive Zoom call among professionals, the process relies heavily on the email + password combination we're all too familiar with. Furthermore, it's a one-to-one transaction where it's difficult to transfer or give these gated experiences.

As previously discussed in the "Changes to Digital Identity" section, with the emergence of digital wallets as your Internet identifier, this all changes. Because now an NFT can act as the key to unlocking these gated experiences. Here are a few examples:

- If you own a Metaverse HQ NFT, then you have access to an exclusive Discord chat group of 1,500 active NFT traders that are all sharing their insights and strategies for investing in NFTs.

- If you own a Bored Ape Yacht Club NFT, then you have access to the BAYC Bathroom, which is a digital bathroom that you can write graffiti on.

- If you own a MetaKey NFT, then you are given exclusive rights to mint future NFT collaborations with other creators they have in the pipeline.

Turning NFTs into access keys works by using tools like Collab.Land or Unlock Protocol, which provide ready-made software for checking people's wallets to ensure they hold the Access NFT they require. Whether that's a private Discord chat group, an article on a website, or a private party in a virtual environment like Decentraland, these tools will "check your wallet at the door" and admit you only if you hold the NFT that unlocks that experience.

This has major implications for media companies that want to monetize their content, communities that want to keep their admissions low, or anyone who wants to build something on the Internet that requires payment. In this transitory period where usernames and passwords are being replaced by NFT access keys, we're going to continue seeing these products be over-monetized. It will feel as though everyone and everything is financializing access to their product, service, or content. However, this period won't last forever. Ultimately, the need to attract users will outweigh the need to monetize you, the consumer, and free NFT access keys will be widespread.

We think the coolest part about it is that these access keys are transferable. If you grow tired of one of the communities mentioned earlier, you can sell it on an NFT marketplace and recoup your investment. In addition, you're also the proud owner of an NFT that you can display and talk about. These are two concepts that don't hold true if you were, let's say, to purchase a digital subscription to *The New York Times*. There is, of course, always the option to create nontransferable NFTs, thus rendering the resale behavior impossible. However, it's simply not in the ethos of Web3 creators right now to limit the transferability of NFTs. This may change when NFTs begin being used to include personally identifiable information (PII) such as a digital health record. For the time being, though, resale transactions and transferability are a major part of what makes the NFT market possible.

Crowdfunding 2.0

Kickstarter manifested the creator economy we know to rule the Internet today. In somewhat of a nod to Muhammad Yunus (the Nobel Prize winner for his concept of microfinance), Kickstarter showed us that a good idea, product, or story should not be stifled by what your local bank manager deems as a sound business plan and a safe investment. No, creators should be empowered by a community. Furthermore, that community can consist entirely of customers who buy something before it even exists.

What we're describing is the idea of crowdfunding. For many of us, Kickstarter was the first time we were ever exposed to crowdfunding. Kickstarter showed that there were hundreds or thousands of people around the globe who experience the same problems and furthermore that there is actually a builder out there who is making a product without those problems.

Kickstarter may not get the shine or accolades it deserves, but an unfathomable number of products have been crowdfunded thanks to Kickstarter. Countless companies have been born on Kickstarter. While there isn't anything inherently wrong with crowdfunding, other than a creator who raises money and doesn't follow through with their promise, NFTs take crowdfunding to the next level. And that level is a sense of ownership in the project you help crowdfund. Effectively, this takes us from traditional crowdfunding to crowdfunding 2.0.

Take Daniel Allan, for example. He's a music producer who has been working in the industry for some time and really thinking through his next move. As opposed to signing with a label and locking himself into how the label wants to grow him, he turned to a platform called Mirror that acts as sort of a crypto-based crowdfunding platform.

Daniel sold half of the royalties to his upcoming album, titled *Overstimulated*, in exchange for advance funds to help him fund the project. He issued 100,000 $OVERSTIM tokens and sold half of the supply, at the convertible rate of 1 ETH = 1,000 $OVERSTIM, which at the time was around $147,000 USD. Furthermore, he created three NFT packages at the price points of 0.1 ETH, 0.25 ETH, and 1.0 ETH, each NFT being composed of a visual collectible, the royalty contract details, and the respective amount of $OVERSTIM tokens.

In just a few days, 87 people purchased an NFT from him, and he raised a total of 50 ETH for his EP. He outlined how he planned to allocate the funds, the timeline for the EP, who was going to be featured, the royalty details, and so on. In the process of crowdfunding money for his project, he simultaneously crowdfunded a community of supporters. Each of these supporters was a marketing vessel. Those NFTs were in their wallets. They'd see them every day and think about how they could help promote and make the album go further. The incentives were all aligned.

The beauty of crowdfunding via NFTs is that all the royalty details are coded into the smart contract. There's no way to cut people out of a deal or cheat anyone. It's public information.

Others have used Mirror to crowdfund e-mail newsletters, such as Dirt. One creator by the name of Emily Segal used Mirror to crowdfund her next novel. Even a documentary called *Ethereum: The Infinite Garden* was funded on the Mirror platform.

Not all crowdfunding efforts come with monetary royalties. In some cases, the NFT fundraising either acts as an access token to whatever is being created or is more benevolent in nature—where holding the NFT is simply a way to show that you were an early supporter.

For instance, Stoner Cats is an NFT-based animated series with a star-studded cast including Mila Kunis, Ashton Kutcher, Vitalik Buterin, and Jane Fonda. They sold Stoner Cats avatar NFTs to fund the series. And only those who own one of the NFTs can watch the episodes.

Another futuristic application of NFTs is Parallel Alpha, which is an NFT-based card game that sold NFT cards for a game that didn't yet exist. The funds raised through the NFT release funded the development of the virtual environments where the card game can take place. And naturally, you must own Parallel Alpha cards in order to play the game.

Overall, issuing NFTs as a means for crowdfunding will continue to be a dominating reason that people purchase scarce digital files. It's a more intimate and dynamic way of crowdfunding as a creator because you're aligning the interests of collectors with your project. And the NFT in your blockchain wallet acts as a continuous reminder that you're part of this crowdfunded mission.

NFTs can trace their roots back many years. As early as 2015, people were minting their digital files onto the blockchain. But it was only in the past year or so that people actually started to care to place a value on said digital assets. It was a behavioral shift.

The fact that people now care to own scarce digital files has major implications for the next evolution of the Internet. It changes how economies in video games function, allowing for players to sell their in-game assets after they've grown tired of them. It changes how we build communities, allowing us to create and reserve experiences for people who own those files. It changes how we crowdfund. It changes how we uniquely define our identities. And this is just the start.

The key here is that scarce digital file ownership builds upon the new layer of digital identity we'll have with our blockchain wallets. And that makes immersive Internet experiences more possible.

Changes to Internet Immersion

In the end, we all want to hang out in places on the Internet where our friends are. We want to connect with people around our shared interests. As those niche communities grow, brands and companies will do anything to get in front of people (their customers) in those environments.

What's become entirely evident is that the shopping mall has been replaced by *Fortnite* and *Roblox*. It's where kids go to hang out and loiter with their friends. Both video games are constantly offering new experiences and ways to upgrade and outfit one's characters. The games collaborate with brands and other media companies to merge what's cool elsewhere on the Internet with an experience in the game.

Travis Scott launched an entire *Astroworld* concert grounds in *Fortnite*. Before Travis, it was the DJ by the name of Marshmello who had a concert in *Fortnite*. Ariana Grande has done the same. Other brands, such as Balenciaga have launched exclusive character skins in the game. Louis Vuitton made a similar play in *League of Legends*. It's likely what spurred Nike to start filing a variety of patents on digital merchandise.

Let's jump over to *Roblox*, a game with a lot more freedom to create and play mini-games within the *Roblox* ecosystem. Following the worldwide success of the show *Squid Games* on Netflix, people began creating *Squid Games* experiences in *Roblox*. One such game counted more than 700 million people who played it. It doesn't take a genius to realize why Netflix shortly thereafter announced plans to roll out Netflix Gaming.

This is the future of Internet immersion: brands and companies showing up in cool ways where people are spending time. The experience of going to the Balenciaga website is vastly different from downloading and wearing one of their outfits in *Fortnite*. The impact to Balenciaga's bottom line is still substantial in both instances, but in the *Fortnite* example, they've created an asset that can exist in perpetuity, making it a future-proofed product.

If we want to talk about the first people who will truly experience a shared virtual world, then it's the youth today who are hanging out in *Fortnite* or *Roblox*. As they age and their tastes refine, their behaviors will still remain. Many may still prefer to socialize in virtual environments. They may prefer to work in the virtual setting. Therefore, capturing the youth is key.

That doesn't mean there aren't new immersive experiences for adults.

When it comes to networking, more connections are now made on places like Clubhouse and Twitter Spaces than on LinkedIn. These audio social experiences are a more intimate way of connecting with people than viewing someone's professional profile and messaging them.

There's the entire idea of a "corporate Metaverse" that a few companies are building. This corporate Metaverse iterates on the virtual work apps like Zoom and Slack. For example, Gather allows companies to build an 8-bit video game style office environment with desks and meeting rooms. Employees access it through their web browser, they walk around and connect with each other through their character, and it integrates live video chat as well to get your meetings done.

Both Facebook and Microsoft previewed new work-from-home features that bring the concept of avatars onto video calls. That way it offers employees a break from Zoom fatigue and also gives them a fun way to customize their avatar.

On an entirely different thread, Tinder showcased an interesting new immersive way to find potential partners. They launched a game called Singles Town, where users were represented by an avatar. They could walk up to other avatars (single people) and spark up a conversation with them.

Overall, the world is growing tired of interfacing with static websites and apps. We want to be wowed again, whether we know it or not. That's the large reason why Facebook has rebranded to Meta and doubled down on immersive environments as a way to reconnect with the people.

But the question remains: what environment will house all of these new immersive Internet experiences?

Everyone uses the example of *Ready, Player One*, the movie that showed us a future where people strapped on a VR headset and could do everything from explore to socialize to game to work to build and more in one discrete place. In essence, it's what a place like *Decentraland* is building. If you watched Mark Zuckerberg's keynote on the rebranding to Meta, you might take the hint that they're trying to build a sort of unified "Metaverse" where all social and professional opportunities take place.

However, in all likelihood, the next immersive Internet experiences will be built in silos.

It Starts with Web3 Communities

The implementation of a siloed Metaverse will likely take shape via Web3 first. This is because creating interesting virtual experiences is far more about the strength of the community you can bring to the space and less about what you do once you're there.

For example, consider The MetaKey. A company has minted NFTs that act as keys to unlocking any experience that the MetaKey team wants to create. They have nearly 5,000 people who own one of their MetaKeys. This gives them the power of creating an experience and delighting 5,000 people whenever they want. They literally get to be the guides and hold all 5,000 people's hands through "the Metaverse." They could create an event hosted on a website and tell people, "Hey, pop up over here; we have this cool virtual event taking place."

Another interesting Web3 community, for example, is MVHQ. The MVHQ team collaborated with another community called Royal Society of Players to create an exclusive poker tournament. Only holders of the tokens in either community were allowed to join this virtual poker night and have a chance at winning a prize. (This could've been a collaboration with a company like Heartland Poker Tour, who is still stuck in Web2.)

Immersive experiences make sense only where a community already exists. It's why Balenciaga went to Epic Games to reach the millions of gamers in *Fortnite*.

Web3 communities will be the curators and onboarders to the new immersive Web. Here's a hypothetical example. Take a food blog like TheSpoon. Let's say they want to begin moving away from the static blog experience to a virtual experience. As opposed to creating an entire virtual environment on their own, they can collaborate with a Web3-ready Foodverse like OneRare. OneRare is building a food-related virtual world where players can engage in all sorts of food-related games and collectibles. TheSpoon can tap into that existing user base and create the next version of their media empire in OneRare's Foodverse. And if TheSpoon wants, they can give access tokens to all of their current subscribers in order to bring them over to this new experience.

In other words, the effort that companies have made to build their current web presence isn't entirely moot. But they need to think about how they can work with future-thinkers who are creating the Web3 equivalent. Ultimately, they must work together to win together.

As I've emphasized throughout this entire chapter, the Metaverse is built in small increments. We're not going to just simply wake up to an entirely new virtual way of engaging with Google Docs, *The New York Times*, or Nike. These experiences will be upgraded and iterated in trial runs. We'll get a small taste here and there.

This entire concept of a shared Metaverse, like *Ready, Player One*, showcased where all of these immersive experiences are accessed in one location is possible, in theory—but only if we can agree on a set of open-source protocols that make this portability between competing Metaverses possible. Surely, Meta would like to be the company to make that come to fruition. But in all likelihood, we'll each get a personal Metaverse before that, in the same way everyone experiences their own personalized Internet of their Own Interests right now.

What's the Metaverse's Interface?

The question that everyone seems to be wondering is "where will the Metaverse be accessed?" Meta believes it is in their Oculus VR headsets. While that may be the unanimous place at some point, realistically the Metaverse will be device agnostic.

Web browsers, mobile phones, and TV screens all work just fine to transport people into immersive experiences.

When I look at a conference like ComplexCon, which has transitioned to the virtual stage possibly better than anyone, that entire "virtual conference" can be experienced through a web browser. And it's incredibly engaging.

Decentraland—which is one of the clear front-runners of creating a virtual world for gaming and socializing—is accessed only through your web browser.

Roblox and *Fortnite*, which are arguably two of the greatest use cases we have of a shared virtual world, are played on TV screens, tablets, and mobile phones.

Contrary to popular opinion, a VR headset or AR glasses are not necessary to fully immerse someone in an experience.

It's important to note that Meta is making a huge bet on VR. And I don't think I could ever bet against Zuckerberg or the amount of money his company is pouring into this endeavor. This is their chance to be the thought leaders once again and introduce the masses to a new technology. They have the user base. But then again, so did BlackBerry, Yahoo, and Nokia. Each brought us a new way of using technology, but they weren't able to sustain their places as the leaders.

Ultimately, the next wave of the immersive Internet must create easy on-ramps for creators to build experiences, and they must design their products in such a way that the same kids playing *Roblox* today will be interested in what they have to offer in a decade.

Preparing for the Metaverse

We're moving toward a more decentralized Internet, one where cookies and tracking pixels are made obsolete by a better form of digital identity management. Big changes are happening to the Web, and you need to be prepared.

The newest buzzword to capture the imaginations of creators and businesses is the concept of "the Metaverse." And everyone seems to be scrambling to define it, strategize for it, and create their own version of the Metaverse. But the problem remains that nobody truly knows what the Metaverse will be.

In the late 1990s everyone thought that the Internet's biggest businesses would be built on premium domains like Pets.com or Computer.com. We later found out that the true Internet giants would be built by enabling information sharing and through building bridges for niche social communities to form. Ultimately the name didn't matter if your brand and your community were strong.

Today, Starbucks' mobile app processes more than 70 million transactions per month, more than most banking apps combined. Who could've predicted that a couple of decades ago?

In all actuality, what we believe the Metaverse will be is probably not what we'll come to experience. That's just a reality of Internet innovation. The best thing you can do is to stay abreast of the changes happening to the Web. Web3 and blockchain wallets. Buying and selling digital files through NFT protocols. Designing immersive experiences atop existing games and virtual worlds. These are the main changes happening to the Internet today.

The upcoming chapters will help you better understand these tectonic shifts. We'll highlight a wide array of creators at all levels who are building the next major changes to experiencing the Web. We'll outline how innovators are thinking about the next iteration of the Internet. We'll make it clear where the gray areas, the gaps, the unknowns exist—so that you can think about how to fill them in.

Every time we replace a behavior with a digital service or experience, we make the Metaverse more real. As a decision-maker, or as someone who has invested considerable time in digital, you need to foresee how digital life is changing for consumers, businesses, and creators alike. After all, our future depends on it.

3

Why You Should Care About the Metaverse Now

Interests carry us to new places and spaces. When we find something that catches our interest, it's as if everything else takes a back seat. We put our blinders up and focus entirely on that interest every single free moment we have. It's often referred to as "going down the rabbit hole" when you get sucked into a new interest.

Then there are what QuHarrison likes to call Interest Geeks, which is the type of person who gets so engulfed in an interest that it becomes obsessive. He considers it a personality trait, to some extent, as Interest Geeks routinely find themselves in cycles of fascination.

What separates an Interest Geek from the average person is the depth to which they dive into an interest. They take an interest and go where no person has thought to go before. They're not afraid of the friction associated with charting new territory because the allure of the interest is so strong.

Millions of people consider the NBA to be a major part of their life. Most of them are perfectly content watching games, listening to post-game analysis on ESPN, and maybe managing a fantasy basketball team. Slightly higher on the NBA interest hierarchy are people who create content about their fascination with the NBA. Maybe it's a weekly podcast, the occasional blog post, perhaps a meme page. But at the top of the NBA interest hierarchy, on a level that only a few occupy, is a YouTuber named JxmyHighroller (pronounced Jimmy Highroller).

JxmyHighroller is one of the few true NBA Interest Geeks. Every week he tells a unique story about the NBA through data. Furthermore, he uses data that is not widely available, to the point where you can't help but wonder how he found it. One week, he's covering the history of brothers who have played in the NBA simultaneously, using analytics to determine which pair of siblings were the most efficient in history. The next week he's tracking every game-winning shot made from half-court or further, associating probabilities to find the rarest buzzer-beater of all time. And then he'll rank every single championship run in history, using dozens of data points to build his case for the most challenging and easiest championships ever won.

JxmyHighroller took NBA fandom to a level that's hard to comprehend, and it's nearly impossible to predict where he goes next. Through movies like *Moneyball*, we've all come to realize how data analytics is changing sports at the management level. But we've never seen anyone use data analytics to tell such compelling stories about a sport.

What JxmyHighroller represents is the idea of an Interest Geek in the truest sense.

Most of us are fairly basic in the interests we choose to pursue. Thus, we benefit from having established communities and resources surrounding the interest. Golf, Jiu-Jitsu, skincare, collecting memorabilia, woodworking, gaming, gardening, fishing, yoga, and so on are all well-formed interests. The path to mastery of these interests has been well-documented by the many people who participate. In other words, they are highly Google-able.

On the flip side, there are rare moments throughout history where an interest has not quite broken through to establish critical mass. The number of people pursuing the interest is small and therefore an opportunity exists.

The Well-Timed Interest Geek

Being an Interest Geek in the right place at the right time can have a huge payoff. To be an obsessive creative during a time when there isn't a lot documented about a given Interest is challenging and at most times discouraging. To see something the rest of the world does not see is hard in and of itself. But to then bet a large chunk of your time on that interest is something that most people would call foolish.

This is coming from coauthor QuHarrison, a guy who built a blockchain-powered digital art marketplace in 2015 (before the term NFT was even established). Believe me, you get called crazy and looked at weird far too often when you're a well-timed Interest Geek. And history is full of these people.

We think about mobile app developers in the early days of smartphones. Apple's App Store was taking shape, going from 500 available apps in July 2008 to 225,000 available apps in June 2010. During this time, "Mobile App Developer" became a role at every tech company. Entire studios popped up geared toward creating games and utilities for smartphones. The mobile app economy was entering public discourse. Then something changed around 2014. Through hearing numerous success stories of one app idea making a person rich, nearly everyone began having an idea for an app. The problem was that most of the resources for building an app weren't geared toward the layperson, the person with no coding experience. Enter one of my favorite Interest Geeks from this period: Nick Walter. Nick lived and breathed apps. He recognized the need for entry-level resources that democratized the ability to create apps. Nick launched his first Kickstarter campaign in 2014 called "How to Make a Freaking iPhone App," detailing how to create apps that enabled in-app purchases, geolocation, social integrations, camera functionality, and all the features you needed. His messaging was simple and fun: "...help you make complete apps that you can put on your phone, show your mom, I don't care what you do with it." For a few years, Nick continued to update these courses as new iOS software was released and introduced new courses for the Apple Watch. From the public data we can see, he helped more than 10,000 people build their first app. What's special about Nick (and others doing parallel courses and walkthroughs during this time) is that he was an Interest Geek who went deep and then brought the knowledge back to the surface level. Instead of hoarding knowledge, he shared. And as a result, he introduced his interest to thousands of other people.

Another great example of a well-timed Interest Geek, to go back to the digital art example, is Beeple (also known as Mike Winkelmann). About 15 years ago, Beeple started a project called *Everydays*. As the name suggests, he set out to create and publish a piece of digital art every day. The initial goal was to get better at making art (the interest part), but it quickly grew into an exploration of what's possible with virtual artistic design (the geek part). Digital art grew from an interest to an obsession to a profession, working for a range of corporate clients on advertisements, stage designs, and anything that digital art could express. Then, in 2020, Beeple hit paydirt. NFTs took off. And his collection of more than 5,000 *Everydays* became a perfect use case for NFTs being a mechanism to reward digital creators. Sure enough, his vast portfolio of *Everydays* was packaged into an NFT, put on the auction block at Christie's, and sold for more than $69 million USD. This wasn't a fluke, as he followed up that sale half a year later with the sale of *Human One*—a hybrid generative sculpture—for $29 million USD. Beeple is an Interest Geek who went deep, stayed productive, and played the long game at a perfect time for digital art. As a result, he's considered a figurehead in this amazing movement of digital creators.

To stick with the theme of well-timed Interest Geeks in technology, let's look at the idea of a technology influencer. Today, when a new piece of technology comes out, we have loads of YouTube tech reviews to turn to: Linus Tech Tips, Unbox Therapy, MKBHD, the list goes on. But back in the early 2000s, consumer tech was hitting an inflection point. Tech optionality was just beginning to take shape, meaning that anyone interested in devices began having a lot more choices to make. Blogs like Slashdot, Gizmodo, and Engadget provided real-time reviews and coverage that made diving deep into consumer tech an actual interest to pursue. But we also weren't aware that over time we'd come to trust the opinions of a person over the opinions of a branded blog. The real winners of this particular interest in consumer tech were the YouTube creators. Marques Brownlee (MKBHD) started his YouTube channel—reviewing technology—in 2008. Today, he has 15.2 million subscribers. His opinion of the new iPhone or Tesla update holds more weight than the opinion of The Verge, Engadget, and TechCrunch combined. MKBHD is a well-timed Interest Geek.

Some may say these folks were just lucky. They discovered a trend before it was trendy and reaped the rewards. However, this diminishes the foresight and the hard work needed to actually capitalize on an emerging interest. Seriously, imagine trying to code a mobile app or a website as a layman before Udemy courses on the topic existed. The skills required to tinker and create when no one is advising you how is like charting open waters without a compass. There's a high likelihood that you're coasting in circles, but there's no way to know for certain.

It's one thing to be an Interest Geek in the right place at the right time. But it's another thing to be a well-timed Interest Geek who is highly productive and willing to push an interest forward. As we addressed in the discussion of Nick Walter and app developers, if you geek out over an interest before it's established, then you face a lot of friction in going deep on that subject. Resources are scarce, which means you'll have to rely on self-guided learning. Software and tools aren't yet designed with your use case in mind, which forces you to experiment with makeshift tools. But the one thing that often is present among these early adopters of new interests is tight-knit communities.

Interest Geeks tend to band together in the early days of an emerging interest, making the experimentation phase more palatable and collaborative. And so that brings us to the Interest Geeks of the Metaverse, a group comprised largely of VR enthusiasts who have been pushing this idea of digital immersion for years, some of them decades.

Interest Geeks of the Metaverse

At the risk of passing over the numerous influential thinkers who conjured up the idea of VR, I will kick off this discussion of the Interest Geeks of the Metaverse with Jaron Lanier.

For the unfamiliar, Jaron Lanier is credited with popularizing the term *virtual reality* in the late 1980s. But to say his contribution stopped at the naming of this technology would be a real shame. Jaron is truly one of the foremost visionaries and practitioners that set VR ideas into motion. After leaving Atari in 1985, he founded VPL Research, Inc., with Thomas G. Zimmerman, which would be the first company to develop and sell VR goggles. Most will credit him with co-founding virtual reality. Even though the VR headsets we use today aren't Jaron's, his fingerprints are all over them. Aside from the actual hardware, Jaron Lanier impacted how we think about VR and some of the dangers of it creating "behavior modification empires." It's difficult to sum up his ideas that span multiple books, written manifestos, TED Talks, and more. However, it's safe to say that all of the following Interest Geeks of the Metaverse were directly (or indirectly) influenced by Jaron Lanier.

This brings us to Michael Potts. He's not a household name, by any means, even for many Metaverse enthusiasts. But he's a representative of the next class of Interest Geeks to follow after Jaron. Michael founded M2 Studio in 2001 to provide virtual design services. The consumer application of VR was not established at this time. However, many Fortune 500 corporations needed architectural renderings and animations for ads, websites, new projects, and so on. Michael's sustained fascination with the Metaverse for two decades, without losing faith, is miraculous on its own. But M2's staying power as a company to find themselves still in operation during the most exciting time for VR is a true miracle. Today, they benefit from experiencing the ebbs and flows of VR. They've seen which ideas work. And now they're among the most trusted agencies when it comes to designing readymade Metaverse environments that clients can plug right into and offer to their audience. Michael represents one of the many Interest Geeks of the Metaverse who found their niche on the services side of things.

Now we arrive at the behemoth Interest Geek on Metaverse products: Palmer Luckey. During his early teens (2005 on), Palmer developed a unique obsession with VR, amassing a collection of 50+ VR headsets, most of which were developed in the

1990s. At that time, he began tinkering with headsets of his own design. Later, he joined BraveMind, which was a project out of a USC research lab, treating veterans with PTSD through VR exposure therapy. His fascination was growing. Then at the age of 19, in his third year of college, he took a break to start a company called Oculus VR. They succeeded in developing headsets that were cheaper, more visually engaging, and consumer-friendly. Oculus quickly caught Facebook's attention, which would purchase them for $2B USD just a few years into its existence.

What Palmer pioneered with the Oculus platform ignited an entire wave of developers to become Interest Geeks in the Metaverse, creating a slew of applications and use cases for VR.

For example, you had comedy Interest Geeks like the Gotham Comedy Club developing a Metaverse application in VR for live comedy shows. For me, it was the first time I experienced live streaming in the Metaverse. I can remember watching the first show and comedians were addressing both the in-person crowd and the crowd in VR simultaneously. It completely shifted my mindset on concurrent hybrid experiences in the Metaverse and meatspace.

The next Metaverse experience on the Oculus that completely took me by surprise was The Thrill of the Fight VR application. It was a boxing experience that showed me the potential of fitness in the Metaverse.

More recently, with the onset of NFTs and the ability to own digital assets, we've witnessed a wave of designers and architects create readymade habitats that people can own, host events, and call their home in the Metaverse. For example, Krista Kim designed a virtual home on the Spatial platform called the Mars House (mentioned in Chapter 1), which made headlines when it sold for 288 Ethereum. Similarly, Cyril Lancelin and Benny Or designed a space called The Meeting Place, which is a meeting grounds in the Metaverse designed without the laws of physics limiting them. The idea was to freely think about architecture in order to inspire group idea-storm with the same freedom of thought.

Of course, we cannot forget about the thousands of creators that design games and spaces in Roblox, which is a sort of Metaverse in its own right. Meep City, Jailbreak, and Adopt Me! are just three of the top games in Roblox, which have each attracted more than 3 billion visits.

Coauthor DJ SKEE produced Paris World in Roblox—Paris Hilton's own virtual oasis for hosting events and throwing parties. After hosting a New Year's Party in Paris World, which had more attendees than Time Square, she said, "I had more fun on a computer throwing this party than doing one in real life. This is the future of partying."

The number of people interested in the Metaverse has grown exponentially in just the past year, and our previous list doesn't even come close to the number of Interest Geeks who have been experimenting here. It's a sample of the variety of ways creators are approaching this new tech platform and the diversity of ideas that can exist in the Metaverse.

If you only read the headlines, then you are only exposed to the Metaverse advancements from big tech companies. You'll miss out on all of the Interest Geeks that have been architecting the Metaverse for years, building experiences and spaces to make this technology more relatable and tactile for visitors. After all, the Interest Geeks of the Metaverse are responsible for helping virtual reality hardware manufacturers like Oculus and HTC keep users engaged.

Interest Geeks Over Power Brokers

We crave announcements from influential figures that they're interested in, and investing in, an emerging market. The validation from an entity who has a lot more to lose than we do is just what we need to convince ourselves that this new, flashy object or opportunity is the future. For the Metaverse, this watershed moment has come from none other than Mark Zuckerberg.

Zuckerberg rebranded Facebook to Meta, aligned the bulk of their marketing around the Oculus VR headset, and pledged a minimum of $10B USD a year for the next several years to Facebook Reality Labs—their division tasked with creating AR and VR hardware, software, and content.

You should care about the Metaverse right now because Facebook said so. At least that is what popular opinion believes.

But these watershed announcements are not the most reliable sources to count on. Sometimes the timing is off. We remember the feeling among tech enthusiasts in 2013 when Google released the Google Glass AR headsets to the public. We thought that that was the Metaverse moment. Alternately, sometimes the entire prediction is wrong. Remember 3D TVs? After Christopher Nolan's *Avatar* broke every movie release record imaginable, TV manufacturers everywhere started investing in producing in-home 3D TVs. Turns out no one cared to have this tech in their home.

In other words, don't base your emerging tech belief system on the movements of influential people or how corporate tech imagines these futures. Metaverse announcements from Facebook, Microsoft, YouTube, Epic Games, Shopify, MasterCard, and so on are important. But it's not the entire picture. Instead, opt for believing in the builders, the future thinkers, and the early adopters. The Interest Geeks of the Metaverse, if you will.

The Jaron Laniers, the Palmer Luckeys, the Michael Potts have been signaling this development for years. What these future-thinkers recognized years ago is that the Internet constantly shifts the primary medium of communication, from code to text to photos to videos. What they ultimately realized is that virtual presence is next, and they've built toward making this future come true.

What I'm driving at is that many of us wait for multibillion-dollar companies to tell us what is next in tech. We waited for Facebook and Roblox to go onto CNBC and talk about the Metaverse to signal that we should care about it. I understand this conundrum. It's a tribal mentality. The average person doesn't have a big enough circle of believers to shift mindsets, whereas those who already influence millions do.

As I was building my argument for why you should care about the Metaverse, I'll be honest, it was hard to not include the aforementioned watershed announcements from Big Tech. Frankly, you should care more about the Metaverse now that Facebook is involved. But it's a belief in the tinkerers, the builders, the early adopters of this technology—the Interest Geeks of the Metaverse—that should ultimately influence your decision to care about the Metaverse.

4

History of the Metaverse

The history of the Metaverse is a chronicle of many interconnected technologies. After all, the Metaverse is a convergence
of everything from digital identities to blockchain to extended
reality (XR) devices and the Internet. Therefore, it's difficult to
tell the story of this still-being-created virtual oasis without
addressing the timeline of virtual reality and XR devices. We
cannot leave out the history of digital-native ownership and the
blockchain. Above all, how can we properly address the Metaverse
without covering the creation of its predecessor, the Internet?

Much like we approached Chapter 2, "What Is the Metaverse?"
where we outlined the many parts that make up the Metaverse, in
this chapter we will approach the history of the Metaverse in multiple parallel timelines, condensed into one story. Don't mistake
the order for how developments influenced one another. Many of
the technologies that make up the Metaverse have progressed in
their own siloes, only now in a position to converge in a virtual

destination called the Metaverse. With that in mind, we're going to separately explore how virtual reality, the Internet, virtual worlds, and the blockchain each developed, and then we'll see how they converged to start to shape the Metaverse.

Now, where do we begin this story?

La Réalité Virtuelle

Let's take a trip to France, where the lineage of virtual reality begins in the most unexpected of places: the theater. Antonin Artaud was an influential writer, theater director, and overall creative individual throughout the 1920s, 30s, and 40s. In a collection of five essays he wrote in the early 1930s and published in 1938 called *The Theatre and Its Double*, we come across the first use of the term *virtual reality* (well, actually the French equivalent: *la réalité virtuelle*).

In these essays, Artaud described theater as "la réalité virtuelle," a virtual reality "in which characters, objects, and images take on the phantasmagoric force of alchemy's visionary internal dramas." In other words, the theater allows us to inflate the powerful scenarios of human experience. But through this imaginative, exaggerated process we learn the true nature of humans.

Was the theater stage the first device to bring us a Metaverse? In some ways, yes. But it's an ambitious assumption for us to make. After all, we doubt that Artaud anticipated those two words extending beyond a way to describe the greatness of theater. So, we won't stretch our assumptions to make the tie between Artaud's ideas and the tech-enabled virtual realities we can explore today. However, Artaud put these two words into the ether. For that, we must give him his flowers.

It was not until 1965 that the concept of a virtual reality headset was written into existence. Ivan Sutherland wrote a paper describing a virtual world created by computer software and accessed by people through a head-mounted device. The "Ultimate Display," as he called it, was literally a headset computer that could control the existence of matter and allow people to interact in novel ways.

That same year, Morton Hellig created a VR prototype of his own called the Sensorama Simulator. He described the device as an "experience theater," and it sounds like it was nothing short of an experience to remember. The Sensorama played 3D film and stereo sound, in addition to pumping in aromas and wind to round out the immersiveness. Naturally, this refrigerator-sized device never found commercial appeal.

Throughout the 1980s and 1990s, the distant future of virtual reality made for great entertainment. William Gibson's novel *Neuromancer* (1984) beautifully defined and coined the term *cyberspace*. Three years prior, Vernor Vinge's novella *True Names* portrayed an accurate vision of cyberspace as well. And as we discussed in Chapter 2, Neal Stephenson wrote the "Magna Carta of the Metaverse" in 1992, *Snow Crash*. Visions of virtual reality also made it to the silver screen during this time period. Most notably, *Tron* explored a virtual realm akin to a Metaverse in 1982. The following year, *Brainstorm* transported viewers to a future where VR devices were an industry and unfortunately being misused. Then in the mid-to-late 1990s we were blessed with two Keanu Reeves classics, *Johnny Mnemonic* (1995) and *The Matrix* (1999), which both explore the idea of virtual or simulated realities.

These fictional versions on virtual reality, especially *Snow Crash*, were instrumental in influencing creators of all types. In an interview with the Academy of Achievement in 2000, Google cofounder Sergey Brin cited *Snow Crash* as a key source of inspiration saying, "[*Snow Crash*] was really ten years ahead of its time. It kind of anticipated what's going to happen, and I find that really interesting." That same year, likely inspired by the visionary thinking on display in *Snow Crash*, Amazon founder Jeff Bezos hired its author Neal Stephenson for his spaceflight company, Blue Origin, where Stephenson held various positions until 2006.

After the Ultimate Display and the Sensorama, flight and space simulators became common for commercial airlines, the military, NASA, and other organizations. Simulators are a version of virtual reality; however, the tech wasn't ever intended to be used for more universal use cases. These were specific "VR" devices for specific applications. However, throughout the 1980s and 1990s, Jaron Lanier was pushing consumer-grade virtual reality device research forward. Among the greatest of his achievements during this time was his performance of virtual reality music instruments (VRMI) during his 1992 performance *Sound of One Hand* in Chicago.

Throughout the late 1990s and early 2000s, many iterations of virtual reality headsets and experiences would be developed— Sega's VR-1 motion simulator, Nintendo's Virtual Boy console, Linden Lab's "The Rig," and the SAS Cube to name a few. Many of these were clunky, expensive, and limited in what they could do. However, many were inspirations for Palmer Luckey, who crowdfunded his first Oculus VR headset prototype on Kickstarter in 2013. As we addressed in Chapter 3, "Why You Should Care About the Metaverse Now," his Oculus tech quickly caught the attention of Facebook and in 2014 was acquired for $2 billion USD.

Before we get too far ahead of ourselves, we cannot forget about the foundation and predecessor of the Metaverse.

The Early Internet

In 1945, American engineer Vannevar Bush envisioned a device called "Memex" in an essay *As We May Think*. His primitive computing device would fit on a desktop and aid users in managing all types of documents and media by compressing and storing them, in addition to corresponding with others.

On August 6, 1991, Tim Berners-Lee introduced the public to the World Wide Web, posting the very first public invitation for collaboration. Thus, the Internet was born.

In between these two dates, the foundation of the Internet was laid. We'll name a few of the great Internet advances during the 1960s and 1970s. J.C.R. Licklider of MIT led the discussion around a "Galactic Network" in 1962, which was a globally interconnected set of computers through which everyone could quickly access data and programs from any site. Leonard Kleinrock at MIT published the first paper on packet switching theory in July 1961, which explored the use of information packets rather than circuits to send communications. This would become a fixture in computer networking. Lawrence G. Roberts and Thomas Merrill built the first computer network in 1965, connecting two computers, one in Massachusetts and one in California, with a low-speed dial-up telephone. Researchers at Brown University started developing the Hypertext Editing System in 1967, which would influence many hypertext iterations and therefore the Internet interfaces through which we accessed information. Above all, there was the DARPA-funded ARPANET, which was undoubtedly the first iteration of the Internet starting in 1969.

There are many people who have documented the history of the Internet in a beautiful and expansive way. You can head over to Internetsociety.org to get your fix of Internet history. Ultimately, we felt trying to create a synopsis for this just wouldn't do it justice. However, we will sum it up in the overarching philosophies that made this era so great.

The early Internet, pre-Tim-Berners-Lee, was largely led by government-funded projects at public and private universities. It was pioneered by researchers who weren't backed by corporations looking for ways to improve their bottom line. Many of the protocols created during this time carry over to the modern Internet.

The result was a free and open Internet that would eventually allow anyone to join and create.

But imagine if the reverse were true, as is the case with the Metaverse development today, and the Internet had been created by corporations. We would've been taxed for every Internet action we took. Many of us might have been deterred from even using the World Wide Web. And who knows what other sort of "butterfly effects" this alternate pathway would've led us down.

Of course, the free and open Internet that we did create has led to all sorts of privacy issues and social problems. But it's difficult to know if the alternative, where we pay a microtransaction for every single Internet click, would be any better. Once we reach the 1990s and we have the Internet, we begin to see the first creations of virtual worlds.

Early Virtual Worlds

In 1995, Active Worlds and The Palace were both developed and launched to the public. While their interfaces were more akin to a chatroom, users were still able to display themselves as pseudonymous avatars, a trend that will continue into the future of virtual world experiences.

In 1998, There.com launched a virtual world-based game that users could explore, socialize in, and even transact purchases or services with the game's currency: Therebucks. As we addressed in Chapter 1, "A Vision for the Metaverse in 2032," There.com (and its developer Makena Technologies) attracted a lot of interest from corporations like Coca-Cola and MTV to build out their own virtual worlds.

In 2001, the Massively Multiplayer Online Role-Playing Game (or MMORPG for short) *RuneScape* was released. By 2012, *RuneScape* had more than 200 million users create accounts and play their game. Fantasy MMORPGs of all types—*World of*

Warcraft, Elder Scrolls Online, MapleStory—dominated the gaming communities throughout the early 2000s and onward. In most cases, we don't consider MMORPGs to be examples of Metaverses because we believe Metaverses must provide a more expansive way of creating within the game. Still, they incorporated virtual worlds and in-game economies that result in real earnings (sometimes) for players. These are two concepts that will find a more substantial existence in the late 2010s and early 2020s with play-to-earn blockchain games.

One game that we would, however, classify as both an MMORPG and an early Metaverse would be Second Life. Created by Philip Rosedale and his company Linden Lab in 2003, Second Life was much like There.com in the complete freedom it offered its user base. Residents of Second Life were given spaces to socialize, participate in both individual and group activities, and build, create, shop, and trade virtual property and services with one another using the Linden Dollar (which can be converted to real-world currency). Second Life proved to be an economic vehicle for its residents early on, with one of its biggest success stories happening in 2006 when Anshe Chung sold her virtual property for the equivalent of $1 million USD in Linden Dollars. Not all economic activities are this massive in nature, though. Other residents found success designing and selling objects like clothing for a couple of dollars a pop or providing services like graphic design and architecture development in the game for varying rates. Within a decade, Second Life had 1 million active users and a GDP of ~$500 million USD. Yes, a virtual world calculated its own GDP. Second Life sets itself apart from other early virtual worlds in its ability to sustain its product and user base over time. Rosedale confirmed in 2021 in an interview with IEEE Spectrum that its community still sits around 1 million users and facilitates about $650 million USD in annual transaction value.

Although Second Life was never able to extend much further than a million residents, another virtual world developed around the same time eventually found viral growth and reached heights for digital economies that we're sure even Metaverse visionaries like Neal Stephenson would be shocked by. That virtual world we're referring to is Roblox.

Roblox was created by David Baszucki and Erik Cassel in 2004 and launched to the public in 2006. Roblox hosts user-created games and experiences, as well as an economy for in-game accessories like virtual clothing and weapons, which they can purchase with its native digital currency Robux. Robux can be purchased with real dollars through their games, but can never be exchanged from Robux back into dollars. Roblox was a relatively small ecosystem until the late 2010s when it saw parabolic growth. The global pandemic positioned Roblox as the perfect place for kids to interact with friends. *The New York Times* reported in August 2020 that the game crossed 164 million users and was played by about 75 percent of all American children ages 9 to 12. Roblox reported that as of June 2021, 1.3 million creators and developers were earning Robux and were on track to earn $500 million USD in 2021.

Naturally, many brands see the lucrative opportunity to reach the youth on Roblox. Companies like Nike and NASCAR have created branded accessories and vehicles for the game. The platform has since expanded beyond just games to a platform for all sorts of immersive experiences, ranging from educational and social spaces to digital parties and concerts. Today, they are consistently referred to as a leading Metaverse platform, which was partly cemented by their IPO in March 2021 (their market cap hovers around $30 billion USD). Now, everyone who watches CNBC regularly knows of two Metaverse companies, Meta and Roblox. And that's a significant signal for the future of their platform.

Through this period, we establish that economies can exist in digital-native environments. There.com, Second Life, Roblox, and a number of other games are proof of this. However, a technology that will be created in 2009 will bring scarcity and a true proof of ownership to these digital assets and services.

Blockchain and Digital Assets

It's safe to say that email was the first widespread use case of the Internet. But email actually predates the modern Web created by Tim Berners-Lee. Back in the days of ARPANET, Ray Tomlinson devised a system of electronic mail that allowed users to leave notes on a computer for the next user. Once it became clear that computer-to-computer communication would be the norm, Ray came up with the @ symbol to actually indicate computer destinations for people to send their electronic mail to. It is perhaps the most enduring Internet invention to this day. And by 1976, 75 percent of all ARPANET traffic was electronic mail.

When we reach the 1990s and the public-facing Internet, it is evident that this widespread use of the Internet (and therefore email) could be used nefariously by marketers to send unwanted spam. To oppose this influx of junk mail, Cynthia Dwork and Moni Naor would come up with the idea "...to require a user to compute a moderately hard, but not intractable function..." in their 1992 paper *Pricing via Processing or Combatting Junk Mail*. In other words, by requiring a computer to do a small amount of work before requesting a service on a network, we might deter bad actors from sending overwhelming amounts of traffic (or emails) in what's called a denial-of-service attack.

This concept would take on the name of *proof of work*, which Adam Back formalized in 1997 with a technology called Hashcash. Hashcash was a proof-of-work system that could be added to email clients to prevent spam. Although Hashcash wasn't widely adopted except in some blogs and a few email clients, it showcased the application of proof-of-work systems. In a decade, we'll really come to understand the potential of proof-of-work.

A parallel advance in cryptography was introduced in 1998, although not for the use in Internet traffic, but rather for the use of currency. Wei Dai revealed his concept for b-money that would be a decentralized, distributed cryptocurrency. While b-money was never created, Wei Dai was one of the early pioneers formulating ways to create native Internet money.

The year is now 2009 and the Internet is blessed with its first blockchain (a digital ledger used to record transactions) and subsequent asset on that blockchain. That asset we're referring to is Bitcoin, the world's first cryptocurrency to utilize a decentralized, distributed blockchain ledger to verify, legitimize, and record transactions of Bitcoin. On January 3, 2009, it's mysterious, pseudonymous creator Satoshi Nakamoto uses a proof-of-work system to mine the first block on the Bitcoin blockchain—an action that yielded a reward of 50 Bitcoins. On this date, Bitcoin is born and with it the wheels of the Metaverse speed up.

With an operational blockchain in existence, innovators begin looking beyond the use case of cryptocurrency to other digital assets. Yoni Assia writes a blog post in 2012 titled "bitcoin 2.X (aka Colored Bitcoin) — initial specs," which envisions cryptocurrency tokens as a way to create, buy, sell, and own unique assets via the blockchain. That same year, Yoni publishes the Colored Coins Whitepaper with four others, including one name we'll become highly familiar with, Vitalik Buterin. The Colored Coins Whitepaper outlines a variety of uses for tokens on a blockchain such as digital collectibles, smart property, issuing shares, creating a community currency, as well as for access and subscription services. Eventually, the colored coins concept will evolve into the label of nonfungible tokens (NFTs). And all of the use cases they outlined will later become fixtures in the NFT market.

One of the earliest protocols to be written on the Bitcoin blockchain was Counterparty. In 2014, Robby Dermody, Adam Krellenstein, and Ouziel Slama launched Counterparty—the first decentralized finance platform that allowed users to mint their own tradeable currencies and assets on the Bitcoin blockchain. *Wired Magazine* published a story in July 2014 outlining how Overstock.com was interested in using a platform like Counterparty to issue the first publicly traded stocks on the blockchain. Overstock (rooted in its CEO Patrick Byrne's philosophy) was among the first corporations to be interested in the potential of cryptocurrency, notably being the first retailer to accept Bitcoin as payment. While Counterparty technically enabled the Bitcoin blockchain to be the hub for all crypto-related development, it was actually the Ethereum network that would take the cake here.

We've established that Vitalik Buterin was tinkering with the blockchain as early as the age of 18, when he contributed to the Colored Coins whitepaper. Was this how famed entrepreneur and investor Peter Thiel discovered Vitalik? We're unsure. Regardless, in 2014, the then 20-year-old Vitalik Buterin was a recipient of the Thiel Fellowship grant. The Thiel Fellowship offers $100,000 USD grants for exceptional students under the age of 22 to leave school and pursue other work. This "other work" that Vitalik was pursuing would be the only blockchain and cryptocurrency to ever rival Bitcoin.

In July 2015, Vitalik Buterin and Gavin Wood launched the Ethereum Network, along with the Ethereum blockchain. In a nod to one of cryptocurrency's earliest visionaries, the smallest unit of an Ether token is named *wei* after Wei Dai. Notably, Ethereum's blockchain was faster and cheaper to build on than Bitcoin's, in addition to the fact that people knew who its founders were and could interface with them. This made the Ethereum Network a friendlier environment for blockchain developers to explore the use of smart contracts and build dApps (decentralized apps). For this reason, many of the first and most impactful blockchain games, NFT projects, and Metaverses were built on Ethereum, which we'll explore in the next section.

You might be wondering whether the Metaverse has to incorporate the blockchain. After all, both Roblox's gaming environment and Meta's VR platforms don't use the technology and they're often referred to as leaders of the Metaverse. But if you subscribe to our idea of the Metaverse, an idea that is shared by many others, then you believe that the Metaverse is a movement toward decentralization—an Internet that doesn't rely entirely on central authorities. Therefore, blockchain is in fact necessary to the Metaverse as it uses a peer-to-peer network of computers to validate each transaction, as opposed to one central company or organization handling all transactions.

That leads us to the modern Metaverse. All of the technology timelines discussed up to this point have converged—virtual reality, the Internet, virtual worlds, and the blockchain—and we've reached a moment where we can begin to see a true Metaverse experience take shape.

The Modern Metaverse

If *Snow Crash* were the novel that inspired the Metaverse creators of the 1990s and 2000s, then Ernest Cline's *Ready, Player One* is the novel that picked up in the 2010s and carried us into the next vision for the Metaverse. Published in 2011, *Ready, Player One* is set in the dystopian future of 2045, where global warming and an energy crisis have caused widespread social problems. Like many people in this era, the main character

Wade Watts lives in slum housing, which consists of shipping containers stacked one atop the other. With few opportunities in the real world, most people turn to a virtual escape called the OASIS, which is accessed through VR headsets and made realistic by full-body haptic feedback suits. Kids go to school in the OASIS because it's safer than the real world. People own businesses in the OASIS because its currency is more stable than dollars. Generally everything enjoyable, social, and of any optimistic outlook happens in the OASIS.

James Halliday, the creator of the OASIS, passes away leaving its billions of users with one last experience of his design—an Easter egg hunt to whom the winner will receive Halliday's entire fortune and control of the OASIS. Watts, whose avatar in the Metaverse is named Parcival, is not only up against all other users but also an evil Metaverse corporation called IOI, which employs an endless supply of avatars in the OASIS. It's a beautiful tale that weaves in a lot of 1980s video game culture and, of course, illustrates the Metaverse.

Ready, Player One went far beyond *Snow Crash* in showing us what the Metaverse could be. Cline does an incredible job painting a picture of the Metaverse in all of its personal and professional possibilities. He depicts how worlds within the Metaverse will differ in design and experience. His book was hugely impactful. But when it was made into a movie seven years later, with Steven Spielberg as its director, this illustration of the Metaverse became even more vivid and real.

A handful of years after the publishing of Cline's book, in 2015, two Argentinian developers begin working on a blockchain-based Metaverse called Decentraland, whose mission was to create something very much like the OASIS in *Ready, Player One*. Ari Meilich and Esteban Ordano choose Ethereum as the blockchain on which all of Decentraland's assets and transactions would be recorded. In 2017, they held their initial coin offering, raising more than $26 million USD in roughly 30 seconds. In Chapter 6, "Enter the Metaverse," we describe Decentraland (and many of its competitors including The Sandbox and CryptoVoxels) in great detail and showcase many fascinating things happening in this Metaverse. We will, however, leave you with one note about how far Decentraland has come. Near the end of 2021, a virtual real estate firm called the Metaverse Group purchased a 116-parcel estate in Decentraland for 618,000 MANA (or about $2.4 million USD at the time).

On a similar Metaverse note, minus the blockchain, in 2016 *Pokémon Go* is released to the public and quickly becomes the number-one game in the United States. *Pokémon Go* was the first game of its kind to overlay an augmented digital world onto the real world. Players used their mobile devices to hunt and capture Pokémon Go, which are placed throughout the real world and found via GPS. Back in 2000, Gartner coins the term *supranet* to refer to the convergence of the virtual and physical worlds in the age of the Internet. *Pokémon Go* is a perfect representation of this supranet that Gartner described.

In the same year that *Pokémon Go* has the first hit in the world of augmented reality experience, we also encounter the very first example of another Metaverse concept known as *decentralized autonomous organizations* (DAOs). The first DAO, aptly named The DAO, was launched and crowdfunded in a token sale in May 2016, setting the record for the largest crowdfunding campaign at the time. The DAO's mission was to set an example for how venture capital could be reimagined as a group-funded and group-controlled VC fund that would invest in companies and grow. Unfortunately, just a month later users exploited a vulnerability in The DAO and stole at least a third of its money. While The DAO quickly died, the concept of DAOs lives on. Many Metaverse companies opt for the DAO structure, in which the collective participants and owners in the company get actual governance rights.

As 2017 rolled around, we finally began to see the 2012 vision of Colored Coins play out in the form of the first blockchain-based digital collectibles. John Watkinson and Matt Hall minted 10,000 NFT avatar characters, named CryptoPunks, onto the Ethereum blockchain. Each CryptoPunk was algorithmically generated from a list of traits that vary in rarity, resulting in some CryptoPunks that are objectively rarer than others. Wikipedia states that the project was inspired by the London punk scenes, the cyberpunk movement, and electronic music artists Daft Punk. However, our personal theory is that its name is a nod to Cypherpunks, an informal cryptographer movement in the 1980s and 1990s which Wei Dai was a member of. Back in 2017, each CryptoPunk was initially minted and sold for less than $50 USD. As of February 2022, you cannot purchase a CryptoPunk on the open marketplace for less than $175,000 USD, while the rarest CryptoPunks have been appraised for well into the nine figures by top auction houses.

Just a month apart in creation, CryptoKitties launched the first NFT-based game. CryptoKitties, like CryptoPunks, are algorithmically generated kittens. However, what made this project unique was that it not only allowed ownership of a digital collectible but also a gamified experience. Owners could breed CrytpoKitties to create new NFT kittens, offering owners a unique way to interact with their digital assets.

While CryptoPunks and CryptoKitties are not the first NFTs to ever be created, they both found widespread adoption long before the NFT craze of 2021. The honorable title of "First NFT Ever Minted" goes to Kevin McCoy and Anil Dash. At a 2014 event called Seven on Seven, the pairing came up with the first way to attribute and track ownership of a digital asset on the blockchain. Their NFT art was titled *Quantum* and sold for a meager sum (to Kevin). To this day, the protocol they designed is used across the NFT landscape.

CryptoKitties offered us the first glimpse of NFT-based games. But it's in 2018 that we were introduced to a model for NFT gaming called *play-to-earn* that truly creates utility for NFTs in games. A startup called Sky Mavis launched *Axie Infinity*, which is essentially a turn-based battle game featuring NFT characters called Axies as the in-game characters. To play *Axie Infinity*, players must purchase three Axie characters. With these NFTs, they can enter the game and begin battling other players or going on quests to earn the in-game currency $SLP (smooth love potion). $SLP can be either traded into other cryptocurrencies or used to breed new Axies, which players can then sell on the Axie NFT marketplace. Axie experienced viral growth in 2021, particularly fueled by adoption in Southeast Asia, growing to more than 1.8 million daily users and generating more than $2 billion USD for their community of players through the game. While play-to-earn technology traces its roots back to the Japanese Gacha games of the 2010s (such as MapleStory), *Axie Infinity* was the first to successfully integrate the model on the blockchain.

When the global pandemic hit in 2020, many people began turning to Metaverse-related platforms for fun and to connect with their friends. Popular games like *Minecraft*, *Fortnite*, and *Animal Crossing: New Horizons* experienced a wave of growth and engagement. We should preface this by saying that while these games are not built with blockchain or NFT integrations, nor accessed through virtual reality games, in some ways they are still modern Metaverse platforms. These games familiarize particularly the youth with digital economies and digital asset ownership within a virtual universe. These will be significant on-ramps to the Metaverse as this cohort of users ages. And we're talking about a large pool of potential Metaverse users here. As of March 2021, *Minecraft* had more than 140 million monthly players. From its inception in 2017 to 2021, *Fortnite* has grown its user base to

350 million registered users, brought in more than $5 billion USD in revenue of digital accessories in 2020, and hosted concerts for Marshmello and Travis Scott that each attracted 10+ million attendees. And in one year's time since its release, *Animal Crossing: New Horizons* has sold more than 32 million units of its game.

But it's not just Metaverse-like games that feel the effects of the pandemic. Toward the end of 2020, the NFT market began ramping up. Notably, Mike Winkelman, a.k.a. Beeple, sold his first NFTs on Nifty Gateway and a few months later in March 2021 sold an NFT collection called *Everydays: The First 5,000 Days* for $69 million USD at a Christie's auction.

In large part, this sale caused the NFT market to absolutely explode. Creatives, developers, and celebrities have swarmed this burgeoning new form of digital monetization. We cannot even begin to scratch the surface of all the notable sales that happened during this time. However, we'll sum it up by saying that more than $20 billion USD was transacted with NFTs in 2021.

Every day, the world becomes more familiar with the Metaverse through a variety of different channels, whether on blockchain games or through virtual reality headsets, buying virtual real estate, building in sandbox environments, or trading NFTs. Each one of these is a puzzle piece that fits into the greater picture that is the Metaverse.

5

The Metaverse Building Blocks

It's no secret that reality TV has become one of the most pervasive and lucrative entertainment formats there is. *Big Brother*, *Survivor*, and *The Real World* proved there was intrigue in watching everyday people on television. *Keeping up with the Kardashians* showed us just how big and influential reality TV could be. Many cable networks in the early 2000s—including Bravo, A&E, E!, TLC, History, VH1, and MTV—pivoted almost their entire programming schedule to reality TV. And just when we think that we've had our fill of our reality shows, a network will drop another spin-off with a slightly different twist.

However, a reality TV twist none of us saw coming was the viewer getting the chance to affect the outcome of a reality show. We're not referring to fan voting on *American Idol* but, rather, a reality show whose entire plot and moving force is in the hands of the collective viewership.

That show was *Rival Peak*. Launched at the end of 2020, *Rival Peak* was an experimental competition reality show, featuring 12 AI contestants whose fate and survival was controlled by the viewers. The whole experience existed on Facebook Watch and consisted of 13 different streams. Twelve of those streams were dedicated to each individual contestant, allowing viewers to follow their favorite (or least favorite) character in a 24/7 live stream and cast votes on an interactive overlay deciding the outcome of certain things such as tomorrow's weather, help or hinder the AI characters in a range of decisions and projects, solve puzzles, and so forth. The 13th stream was a weekly recap show called *Rival Speak*, where its host Wil Wheaton would sum up and react to what happened to the contestants.

The clearest way to describe the show was like *Survivor* meets *The Sims*. This new show format was imagined and created by a trio of specialist companies—game developer Pipeworks Studios, interactive broadcasting company Genvid Technologies, and Hollywood production firm DJ2 Entertainment.

This was not some hole-in-the-wall production that nobody paid attention to. No, *Rival Peak* garnered streaming numbers that rival that of the biggest TV shows and surely surpass most of the content on Netflix. Throughout its 12-week season, viewers cast millions of votes to impact the show. The combined 12 contestant streams racked up a collective 100+ million minutes watched. *Rival Speak* averaged 12 million views per episode, ending with a total 155 million views. But perhaps the most notable figure is that the minutes watched were more than 55x greater in week 12 than in week 1, showing how much this program grew in influence over time.

So why are we talking about this reality show featuring responsive AI contestants? What does it have to do with the building blocks of the Metaverse?

For one, it proves that when it comes to "reality" entertainment, we have no problem accepting a program where the subjects are nonreal avatars, which means a lot for what television in the Metaverse might look like. Two, it's a showcase of the type of content we can create through Metaverse-building tools like Unity Technologies.

Avatar-led entertainment is a fascinating trend that has been running parallel to Metaverse development for some time. Bear with us, this will all make sense in the grand scheme of this chapter.

In the United States, Lil Miquela took the world by storm starting in 2016. She's a 19-year-old digital human (or avatar) obsessed with fashion whose entire existence lives on an Instagram feed. Well, that was until her influence grew to more than 3 million followers and brands took notice, featuring her in fashion ads alongside real models for Vogue, Calvin Klein, and Prada. Lil Miquela then followed the path of many Instagram-famous influencers, dropping her own clothing line, starting a music career, and directing a documentary short about her life.

But the original digital human to go big was Hatsune Miku. For a long time, Hatsune was one of Japan's most famous pop-stars, counting more than 2 million people in her fan base. Notably, she's been an opening act for both Lady Gaga and Pharrel. But if you type her name into Google, you'll notice something odd. She's not (physically) real. When she performs on stage, she relies on holograms to give her presence. Hatsune Miku was the first virtual popstar and furthermore set a very high bar for future virtual popstars to come. Interestingly, Hatsune was created by Crypton Future Media in order to sell vocal synthesizing software to the music industry. They designed her as a showcase of the product's abilities. In that sense, Hatsune Miku was the first virtual brand ambassador. It's a visionary idea even by today's standards, let alone during her initial release in 2007. Vocal software aside, Hatsune Miku has filled venue seats for more than a decade and counting. And that's what makes her so fascinating.

It's evident that we have no problem being entertained by digital beings. This means a lot for anyone who holds significant IP of video games, cartoons, or animated movies. Imagine what could be done with Metaverse meet-and-greets. Rick from *Rick and Morty* and Cartman from *South Park* have massive fan bases spanning years of entertainment. We also think about all of the nonplayer characters (NPCs) in video games such as Professor Oak from *Pokémon*, GLaDOS from *Portal*, or Cortana from *Halo*. People would love hanging out and spending a day with these avatars. If *Rival Peak*'s avatars, to which we had no previous attachment, could attract 100 million minutes of engagement, then what would happen if the same experiment was done with all of Disney's iconic protagonists?

As we look at the type of Metaverse entertainment that will come to be created and dominate attention, avatars open us up to a lot of possibilities. Ultimately, *Rival Peak* gave us an entirely new way to think about how cartoons or animated movies might find a second life in the Metaverse.

We are leaning into *Rival Peak* and the subject of avatars for two reasons. First, *Rival Peak* was designed in Unity—arguably the leading tool for designing 3D spaces, objects, and other Metaverse assets. Second, avatars, NPCs, and digital twins are a major part of Unity's business. With that being said, let's get into the tools used to build the Metaverse.

The Main Metaverse Tools

Back in 2018, two-thirds of all augmented reality (AR) and virtual reality (VR) apps were built with Unity Technologies. We can safely assume that most of the other third belonged to Epic

Games' Unreal Engine. While we couldn't find a figure that states the market share today, if you talk to any game developer, extended reality (XR) app builder, or 3D designer, they are likely going to mention their use of one of these two tools.

Unity and Unreal Engine are 3D creation tools used to design and render 3D content in real time. They've found market share in industries from film to video games to architecture to automobiles and just about anything that requires 3D design. To show just how impactful these tools are, here's a small sample of the variety of ways Unreal Engine has been used. Everyone knows of Epic Games' *Fortnite*, which naturally uses their own Unreal Engine. But if you head over to Wikipedia and type in "List of Unreal Engine games," you'll find a list that numbers close to a thousand games (we didn't care to count). Outside of games, though, Unreal Engine was used for both hit TV series' *The Mandalorian* and *Westworld*. During Hurricane Florence in 2018, The Weather Channel used Unreal Engine to create a realistic visualization of what the storm surge would bring to a common neighborhood. Even pharmaceutical companies have used Unreal Engine to visualize and manipulate 3D molecules for research.

Getting back to the topic of avatars, one of the most interesting places that Unity has taken their technology is in the field of simulating the actions of nonplayer characters (NPCs). Everyone who has played a video game knows what an NPC is. They are the beings that populate games by operating storefronts, telling us our next quest, and doing literally anything to help the game's story move forward. But Unity also realized how effective NPCs could be for business use cases. In a 2022 Wired article, Cecilia D'Anastasio framed this in terms of describing roller coaster design (www.wired.com/story/gaming-giant-unity-wants-to-digitally-clone-the-world). She pointed out that engineers can't have real people stand up hundreds of times on sharp turns to see whether they'll fly out of a roller coaster car. But they can put NPCs who have the height, weight, motion, and behavioral attributes of a human being on a digital roller coaster. They can even factor in variables for multiple passengers, aging structure, and more. D'Anastasio explained, "Unity spun that idea into an arm of its business and is now leveraging its game engine technology to help clients make 'digital twins' of real-life objects, environments, and, recently, people."

Whereas Unity and Unreal Engine were once in the business of providing graphics software for video games, they now find themselves in the business of simulation.

Digital twins was a concept first introduced by Michael Grieves in 2002. The idea was that we could create a digital counterpart of all physical objects in order to assist with product lifecycle management. Today, digital twins are a core part of Unity and Unreal Engine's business.

These software suites train artificial intelligence to make digital twins act and behave near perfectly to the realism of the world—including everything from how rust forms on metal to how a "human" will react if a car swerves in their direction. This simulation software has major implications.

For example, The Hong Kong International Airport was famously designed using Unity, which they chose for its simulation abilities. In the design process, they could stress-test it for a variety of emergencies—from fires to floods to power outages—to see how the flow of humans would play out during these worst-case-scenario situations.

Because Unity's technology is accessible to so many people, we will surely see their work with realistic digital twins parlayed into the Metaverse. If we go back to the *Rival Peak* example of reality TV centered on AI characters, Unity and Unreal Engine will help this type of content feel more real. And this is true not only for reality TV in the Metaverse. Metaverse social apps, games, workplace environments, and so on will all be made more real through these two simulation engines.

We outline all of these examples in order for you to understand that the Metaverse's building blocks rely heavily on Unity and Unreal Engine. Obviously, almost none of the aforementioned examples is meant to operate as explorable, public Metaverses. But because they're built in Unity or Unreal Engine, they very well could be deployed to millions of devices if their creators so choose.

Outside of designing beautiful 3D environments and objects, that's the true benefit of these two tools. They have interoperability built into their software.

If you're a game developer or XR developer, then you are often met with the hard decision of choosing which platform you're going to build your product on. With a handful of different device types—smartphones, gaming consoles, VR headsets, and PCs—in addition to the disconnectedness of software standards, developers are often met with the paradox of choice. There are too many platforms to build and deploy on, with not enough resources to solve them all.

However, Unity and Unreal Engine solve this interoperability problem, making it easy for developers and designers to design once and deploy almost universally across device and file types. In this sense, they operate as the translation layer for the Metaverse. You input the variables you need in your designs, and they modify the files to fit the requirements.

In a 2020 interview with the *LA Times*, Epic Games CEO Tim Sweeney perfectly encapsulated the push toward the interoperability of gaming environments. He explained that the old perspective that competitors needed to close off their platforms from each other had evolved with Fortnite to a point where

Xbox, PlayStation, and Switch players could play together across platforms. This increased usage for all the platforms, demonstrating that there is greater advantage and opportunity when everyone works together.

Although Tim was mostly referencing video games, because their software (and Unity's) is used in so many fields, it's an observation that applies to the Metaverse at large. This philosophy of interoperability is crucial to making an open and connected Metaverse real.

While a significant portion of 3D design takes place on these two platforms (and if you want to get into designing Metaverse experiences you should definitely check them out), we caution you not to assume that they're the only options out there.

The Secondary Metaverse Tools

Because 3D modeling is used in so many industries, a variety of software suites have been created to solve the specific needs in a given industry. Over the years, the lines have blurred on what use cases these tools are for. However, here's a general consensus on what industries use what tools for designing 3D models and rendering digital representations:

- AutoCAD—Architecture
- Autodesk Maya—VFX for film and TV
- Blender—All-in-one tool for modeling, rendering, and animating 3D graphics
- Cinema 4D—Adding motion to 3D designs
- ZBrush—Digital sculpting for avatars

This is just a short list of all the tools to get you started. So don't just take our word for it. Do your own research to find the tool that fits your needs. For commercial applications, creators often design their assets using these and other tools and then bring them over into Unity or Unreal Engine, where they can coordinate many assets in a full environment and deploy their product to millions of devices.

We'd also like to note that the file standards for the Metaverse aren't set in stone. You don't have to commit to a Unity, Unreal Engine, or any other specific tool to get your desired outcome. There are many open source standards for immersive design that allow you to hop in and start building without having to commit to one corporate product or paying the corporate tax. For instance, Epic's Unreal Engine takes a 5 percent cut of all gross revenue on applications that use their engine after they've crossed $3,000 USD per quarter in revenue.

In the following list, we run through many of these open source standards and interchange formats for the Metaverse, as well as include a link to learn more about each one:

OpenXR is a royalty-free standard for deploying an interoperable XR app that works across many devices and XR formats. (Learn more at www.khronos.org/openxr).

WebXR is a JavaScript application programming interface (API) that enables developers to render their XR apps for many devices including the HTC Vive, Oculus Rift, Google Cardboard, and Open Source Virtual Reality. (Learn more at https://immersiveweb.dev).

WebAssembly (Wasm) is a binary instruction format that aims to create consensus across the many XR file languages. More than 20 languages compile to WebAssembly: Rust, C/C++, C#/.Net, Java, Python, Elixir, Go, and, of course, JavaScript. (Learn more at https://webassembly.org).

XR Engine provides an end-to-end framework and visual editor for building games and social Metaverse experiences, designing avatars, and linking your Metaverse's assets to the blockchain. (Learn more at www.xrfoundation.io).

VRM is a file format for hosting and embedding information, such as personality traits, into 3D avatars. (Learn more at https://vroid.pixiv.help/hc/en-us/articles/360011649274-VRM).

WebGPU is the working name for a web standard and JavaScript API that will enable people with less-than-ideal GPU power to have modern 3D graphics and rendering abilities. It's not yet available. (Learn more at https://en.wikipedia.org/wiki/WebGPU).

Dat is a data-sharing protocol that distributes and hosts data across a network of computers, allowing creators to handle large amounts of data (which is required for Metaverse-building) without stressing their hard drives. (Learn more at https://docs.datproject.org).

IPFS (The InterPlanetary File System) is a protocol and peer-to-peer network for storing and sharing data in a distributed file system. You might know about IPFS from the nonfungible tokens market, where oftentimes NFT creators will host the contents of an NFT using IPFS. (Learn more at https://ipfs.io).

The benefit of designing in these standards is that they're open source and made better by their community of creators. In other words, it's like the difference between Wikipedia and Encyclopedia Britannica. On one hand, the open source standards (like Wikipedia) benefit from faster development updates, whereas the corporate products (like Encyclopedia Britannica) deploy software that has been stress-tested many times over to create the exact product they want to deploy.

Building Your First Metaverse Asset

We're not going to beat around the bush here. There's a steep learning curve to these tools. Building an impressive Metaverse experience is not to be taken lightly.

We look at a concept like the Brooklyn Netaverse, which is the Brooklyn Nets basketball team's way of entering the Metaverse. It's a real-time, 3D stream of home games that allows VR users to watch games from anywhere on the court. It's a far cry from earlier NBA games in VR, where you're given just a couple of unique courtside camera angles to watch the game from. The Netaverse is literally scanning all 10 players on the court and rendering them in a VR environment in real time. To achieve this experience, they are rendering footage from more than 100 high-resolution cameras surrounding the court at Barclays Center and splicing them together onto a virtual court. There's no off-the-shelf software for putting together a Metaverse like this.

Your first Metaverse doesn't have to be this elaborate, of course. You can start with a simple 3D object like a desk, headphones, or whatever you want to create. You can create digital twins of your organization's physical products and avatars of your team. Just know that creators are pushing the boundaries, and currently it takes a lot to be impressive. But don't get bogged down worrying about being impressive. The important thing is to show up first and get your feet wet. Once you get started, you'll have a better idea of how to further develop and improve your Metaverse project.

A how-to manual on creating your first Metaverse could be an entire series of books in and of itself. The tools and resources listed in this chapter are where you can start your research.

You should find solace in knowing that these tools will get easier and more user-friendly over time. In an interview with

"The Information" (www.theinformation.com), John Riccitiello, CEO of Unity, said that he expected some type of AI to be the greatest technological breakthrough in the near future, not a hardware platform. He expects AI-assisted artistry to enable developers to create much better 3D environments than they could create on their own.

Until we reach the day where you can ask AI to design a 3D environment for you, getting your hands dirty is the only way forward with creating your first Metaverse.

6

Enter the Metaverse

Robert Doyle was a career real estate agent before he took a 180-degree turn and began speculating on virtual land and Metaverse businesses. The irony in that statement is too real. Doyle is one of the many early Metaverse adopters whose competitive advantages are simply being interested in the new technology, diving deep into learning about emerging projects, and putting their money where their mouth is.

We should note that Doyle isn't your average crypto-Joe. He operates more than 500 blockchain nodes, has invested in nearly 200 crypto projects, and runs a crypto advisory firm. So he's not a novice by any means. But his story is not too different than many others who have entered the Metaverse before the masses.

Doyle was featured in a *Business Insider* article for the unique assets he acquired in a Metaverse called Polka City. Polka City aims to be the "*Grand Theft Auto* for cryptocurrency"—a reference to the wildly popular video game franchise that revolves around rising through the ranks of a system to develop power. Like most Metaverse projects, Polka City sold NFTs of their in-game assets before the game was developed. They did this in order to fund the immense undertaking of designing a video game. These in-game assets ranged from jetpacks and taxis to hot dog stands and gas stations.

When Polka City announced that minting these NFTs was underway, Doyle had his sights set on the revenue-generating assets. Specifically, he purchased a car repair shop for $23,000 USD and a bank for $3,500 USD. When Polka City is a fully functioning game, these two businesses will generate revenue at a predetermined rate—the car repair shop at 3,750 $POLC per week + 0.00001% for every citizen, while the bank splits a 25% share of all the bridge fees of people converting another crypto into $POLC.

Robert Doyle is a small business owner in the Metaverse. Even though Polka City is in development, like a strategic speculator who buys land in a booming area of town, his assets are already appreciating based on the demand for this Metaverse. The appreciation on these assets alone has netted him nearly $100,000 USD. These profits are held in $POLC—the game's currency—which he could, of course, liquidate. But like so many others, he's here for the long game.

Doyle is just one of the many early Metaverse adopters who is finding fringe opportunities across the landscape of different Metaverses out there. These are not all blind bets. With the right due diligence on the development team, the strength of the community, and their ability to deliver on the roadmap, people like Doyle are finding diamonds in the rough. Now, these diamonds' worth is still speculative. But they're diamonds nonetheless.

Naturally, it's hard to dispute that the majority of Metaverse early adopters are looking for financial incentives. But we caution you from assuming it's the only reason that people are entering the Metaverse.

For example, what was the financial incentive for Ryan and Candice Hurley to get legally married in Decentraland?

The Hurleys had an interest in Decentraland and the Metaverse that they explored often. Therefore, their incentive was the precedent they set by paving the way for a new Metaverse use case. They will go down in history as the first wedding on a blockchain-based Metaverse platform, joining the ranks of two other notable blockchain marriage proposals. The Disney World Bitcoin Conference in 2014 hosted the first blockchain wedding, writing "For better or worse, 'til death do us part because the blockchain is forever." onto the blockchain. Second, in 2021, a California couple who worked at Coinbase wrote a smart contract on Ethereum to issue tokenized "rings" as NFTs during their wedding. The Hurleys are now added to the canonical history of blockchain weddings. By being Metaverse early adopters and taking the risk on their idea, they've reignited the vision of a world filled with virtual weddings. The Hurleys exemplify the behaviors of Metaverse Interest Geeks discussed in Chapter 3, "Why You Should Care About the Metaverse."

Related to this, there's a long-term opportunity for Rose Law Group, who handled the legality of this marriage and hosted the wedding on their Decentraland property. Cointelegraph described their work on the project:

> The law group developed a "meta-marriage framework" by incorporating a "Virtual Premarital Agreement," which identified the couple's virtual identities and digital assets as recorded on the blockchain. Meanwhile, a "Meta-Marriage License" identified, recorded, and tokenized the couple's virtual identities and place of marriage on the blockchain as a nonfungible token.

Rose Law Group is vying to establish the virtual wedding industry—a concept that could make marriage as accessible as tying the knot in Las Vegas and as limitless as the Metaverse is.

They benefit from the knowledge learned through coordinating this event. Not only did they face challenges regarding the legality of this digital marriage (which may not be legally binding), but they also faced technical difficulties in handling the 2,000 attendees. The team that will win the market for virtual weddings will surely be the ones who've experimented the most, understand where the friction lies, and formulate resolutions for all of these hurdles.

Lastly, let's not forget about the 2,000+ attendees who can say they were at the first Meta-Marriage in Decentraland. As thanks for attending, some (not all) were given a POAP NFT to show they were there. POAPs, which are a proof-of-attendance protocol, are tokens that prove you experienced a blockchain-based event. There's an entire subgenre of NFT collectors who simply like amassing proof that they were early adopters of the Metaverse.

As you can see in just this one Metaverse use case, there are multiple motivations for each of the participants. The one common throughline for all of them, though, is the Metaverse event they co-experienced. Each participant now has another reason to talk about Decentraland. Each participant has a story to share with others who don't understand the value of the Metaverse. That's what makes these current moments of experimentation so special.

The purpose of this chapter is to show the wealth of people building experiences in the Metaverse and the variety of use cases they're creating. We want you to understand that there are more ways of getting involved in the Metaverse at this point than simply buying some property there. Yes, getting involved can be just investing. But it can also be as simple as buying a VR headset and exploring a virtual equivalent of your interests like poker, networking, or brain games. If you want to go deeper, you can find developers and design your own space. You can go even deeper and work with companies like Boson Protocol (which we'll discuss later in the "Decentraland" section) to literally build an e-commerce store in Decentraland that will deliver physical products.

The point is that there's more than one way of entering the Metaverse right now. And this chapter will cover a wide variety of use cases from the practical to the possible to the downright visionary.

Not all Metaverses are created alike. So we've first organized the Metaverses by overarching category, with use cases to color in the possibilities in each. The Metaverse categories are as follows:

- **Sandbox Metaverses:** Open platforms that allow for a high degree of freedom in what users can build, how they express themselves through their avatars, and what they purchase through in-game economies.

- **Gaming Metaverses:** Virtual video game environments with clear goals and missions for players, but also featuring economies for players to earn in the game.

- **Miscellaneous Metaverses:** Platforms that don't fit any of these categories but offer a unique experience that will likely be integrated across other Metaverses.

Of course, most Metaverse platforms don't fit nicely into any single box, but rather incorporate bits and pieces of each category.

What you'll quickly come to realize is the amount of optionality in Metaverse platforms you can try. This optionality makes it unwise to invest oneself entirely into one platform. Some people believe highly in the outlook of certain Metaverses, like the DCLblogger who has built an entire brand and business around Decentraland. But when you're in the learning phase, it's best to try a few different platforms.

Ultimately, there are fringe Metaverse opportunities everywhere, as long as you're eager to try new things. With that being said, let's dive into the different ways you can begin entering the Metaverse today.

Sandbox Metaverses

Sandbox Metaverses trace their lineage back to sandbox video games. The term, of course, gets its name from the nature of a sandbox that allows kids to create whatever they want within the confines of the sandbox. Sandbox games, think *Minecraft* and *Roblox*, provide players with an open world to explore and create. Although sandbox games give users tools and assets that are the foundation of the experience, there is no predetermined goal set by the game's developers. In that sense, a sandbox game's sole mission is to inspire creativity. It's like a deck of cards. The structure is set. There are only 52 cards and a couple of jokers. But how you choose to play with that deck of cards is entirely up to your imagination.

You can say that sandbox games, in a way, crowdsource the game's development. This enables sandbox games to grow by network effects. Every time a user creates a new game or event within a sandbox environment it becomes an opportunity to attract new users, while also giving existing users another reason to spend that extra hour in the game.

Where sandbox Metaverses differ from sandbox games is in their integration with a blockchain. All of the land and assets within a sandbox Metaverse are minted as NFTs and tracked on the blockchain. This provides a true sense of ownership and scarcity for in-game accessories and digital assets.

Sandbox Metaverses market themselves as uncharted territory and the freedom to stake one's own space and create whatever you desire on your land. Whereas ownership is the driving force, it's the promise of community that is the retaining feature.

Although there doesn't yet exist a true Metaverse in the sense of a MirrorWorld where every single economic driver in the real world now exists in a virtual world, sandbox Metaverses are the closest thing we have to "the Metaverse." Because sandbox Metaverses provide so much freedom to their users to create what they want, they also have the most creators building unique things. We can't discuss all of them, but we will explore some of the most prominent and interesting ones. So buckle up and let's venture into the first of many sandbox Metaverses.

Decentraland

Decentraland benefits greatly from being the earliest blockchain-based Metaverse, in addition to being up and running at a time when most Metaverses are not. That provides us with a wealth of information to explore in this section.

When Ariel Meilich and Esteban Ordano started the project in 2015, their goal was to create a platform owned entirely by its user base and developed based on the ideas of the community. While the primary narrative shared by the mainstream media is that Decentraland is one of the many Metaverses capitalizing on an absurd digital land boom, Decentraland was not created at a time when people cared about buying digital assets. Instead, it was created at a time when we all collectively worried about the Big Tech platforms owning and controlling too much of our digital livelihood.

Decentraland (DCL) is a browser-based virtual world that currently allows exploration of Genesis City—the first map in DCL. Genesis City is composed of 90,601 plots of user-owned land that are connected by public roads and loosely themed by districts. Districts are meant to organize the types of experiences, businesses, architecture, or owners that inhabit the areas. For example, some of the larger districts include Aetheria (cyberpunk district), Vegas City (gambling district), Festival Land (music district), Battleground (gaming district), and Fashion Street (shopping district).

Aside from the land and every object in this Metaverse having the potential to be a scarce asset represented by NFT ownership, Decentraland is unique in that no single entity or corporation can decide the future of Decentraland, not even its founders. Rather, this Metaverse's development decisions are handled by the Decentraland DAO (which stands for "decentralized autonomous organization"). From their website, it states that "The Decentraland DAO owns the most important smart contracts and assets that make up Decentraland—the LAND Contract, the Estates Contract, Wearables, Content Servers, and the Marketplace. It also owns a substantial purse of MANA, which allows it to be truly autonomous as well as subsidize various operations and initiatives throughout Decentraland."

Users who hold either LAND (Decentraland's plots of land) or $MANA tokens (Decentraland's currency) are given an amount of voting power (VP) respective to their share of assets held. With their VP, users can then govern proposals for DCL. If you visit https://governance.decentraland.org, you'll find a long list of active proposals. Some of these proposals are as simple as asking to put a certain location as a "Point of Interest" on the official DCL map, while others are more complex and ask for a grant to build out their idea.

For example, a play-to-earn game called Decentraland Snap was proposed by Yemel Jardi and meant to incentivize DCL citizens to become virtual photographers. It's a weekly contest where photos or videos taken in Decentraland are entered into a competition for prizes. The proposal talks about how this could help

Decentraland as a whole create more user-generated content to share with the world, in addition to creating an economy for collecting and valuing Decentraland photography native to the platform. Yemel and his team asked for a $5,000 USD grant to build out the tech needed for the project, which ultimately received 85 percent approval from the DAO.

We want to make it clear that every experience in Decentraland does not have to go through this governance approval process. If you own a parcel of land, then you can build whatever you'd like there (within the software limits). For beginners, they offer a Builder Tool with premade assets you can drag and drop onto your parcel. For the advanced, the Decentraland SDK offers more optionality for importing the 3D assets you've created. As we'll address shortly, there are many ways to build in DCL.

In an interview with NBCNews, Sam Hamilton, the head of community and events for the Decentraland Foundation, describes, "The underlying philosophies of Decentraland are for the people to take back control of the internet and decide in which directions it goes," Hamilton said. "The way I see it personally, it's the next generation of social platform."

When you enter Decentraland for the first time, whether as a guest account or via connecting your Ethereum wallet, you'll probably notice the sparseness of the world. You aren't being inundated with stimuli like when you open Instagram. It doesn't seem like a lot is going on. It's difficult to know where to go or what to do. Finding another person to speak with takes time. And getting them to speak to you is another challenge in and of itself. For these reasons, many first-time visitors instantly write Decentraland off.

To Hamilton's point of it being "the next generation of social platform," you might question how it could possibly be a social platform without a lot of socializing going on. How will this Metaverse replace the current Internet destinations we all visit?

First, "replace" is the wrong way to think about these Metaverse platforms. "Extend" is the better word. Decentraland extends the current communities, interests, or experiences we gather around—whether these are digital or physical in nature.

Although Decentraland crossed 500,000 monthly active users in December 2021, at any given time they average just a few thousand concurrent active users. This means that experiencing DCL to its fullest potential is less about wandering around and more about going there with a clear purpose at the right time. In our opinion, the best way to experience Decentraland is through the https://events.decentraland.org page. Here you'll find all of the current and future events going on. Because so much of Decentraland is undeveloped, using this page to port directly to places that have been developed and are running an event makes for a better first experience.

During the last week of March 2022, in partnership with UNXD, Decentraland hosted the Metaverse Fashion Week (MVFW). The goal was to create a digital stop on the global fashion week tour that is more accessible to the global crowd. MVFW incorporated all of the same experiences we expect from a Paris or New York Fashion Week—runways, afterparties, and pop-up shops—except in the digital destination of Decentraland.

Hugo Boss, Tommy Hilfiger, and other major brands participated in MVFW. With the help of companies like Threedium who specialize in scanning physical objects into digital 3D file formats, these brands outfitted their model avatars in digital wearables that reflect their physical garments. And some of them even commercialized their digital fashion, selling NFTs of the garments for players to equip in Decentraland.

The larger trend they're experimenting with is determining whether NFT fashion can be a new revenue stream in Metaverses like DCL, but also operate as a digital storefront for their physical fashion lines. To test this theory, the fashion brands partnered with a company called Boson Protocol, which is creating a means for virtual commerce to deliver physical products. Boson is creating an almost trustless protocol that enables smart contracts to exchange crypto assets for services, goods, digital products, as well as physical products while minimizing the need for intermediaries.

In other words, consumers can purchase an NFT in the Metaverse and redeem the digital asset for a physical product or service. While the Boson Protocol is their smart contract system, the actual product is the Boson Portal. The Boson Portal is a fully customizable brand platform for hosting Metaverse commerce right alongside virtual events and experiences. Think of the Boson Portal as a Shopify store for the Metaverse.

Should Boson or another company prove this tech to be efficient and easy to use, they effectively will have created an e-commerce bridge where Metaverse users can shop both for their avatar and for their physical selves in the same Metaverse environment. You can imagine the idea of a Metaverse shopping mall where we browse stores, make impulse purchases, and receive these goods at our doorstep.

Decentraland's fashion district is already lined with companies who are sitting on virtual properties waiting for Metaverse commerce to take off. Today, if you take a visit to Fashion Street on the far west side of Genesis City, you'll see the beginnings of what could become a Rodeo Drive type of fashion destination. The street is lined with advertisements from the most recognizable fashion brands: Chanel, Dolce & Gabbana, Tommy Hilfiger, and so on. But there's no shopping going on. You cannot enter the buildings. There's nothing to click on or buy. It's a ghost town waiting for the gold rush to come. Still, companies are taking major bets on DCL's fashion district. The Metaverse Group, a subsidiary of Tokens.com, notably scooped up a 116-plot estate in the fashion district for nearly $2.5 million USD. Republic Realm is building a shopping center called Metajuku on a 259-plot estate near Fashion Street, which they feel could become the epicenter of Metaverse commerce. Metajuku already rents space to JPMorgan.

For fashion, the major question still remains whether people will want to do their shopping in the Metaverse. One area that hasn't encountered this problem is the gambling industry.

Located not far from Fashion Street is Vegas City—the gambling hub in Decentraland. Naturally, these two districts are just a stone's throw away from one another, separated only by District X (the red light district, which is apparently where some people spend their casino winnings). So while Republic Realm has bought a large estate in Fashion Street, Boson Protocol has bought an entire block in Vegas City and will be opening shopping centers there too.

The main difference between the fashion district and the gambling district is that the gambling district is in operation and people are using it. The leading team in Vegas City is Decentral Games (not associated with Decentraland), which owns various casino properties in DCL including Tominoya Casino, Atari Casino, and the ICE Poker lounge. Back in February 2022, *Business Insider* reported that over the last three months Decentral Games brought in more than $7.5 million USD in gambling revenue. Not only that, but they also account for a third of the active users in Decentraland.

Gambling has been one of the few verticals to show monetary traction in the Metaverse. Decentral Games' properties are fully functioning casinos that will deal you hands of blackjack and spin the roulette wheel. Furthermore, they're a case study on effectively incorporating NFTs and digital assets with Metaverse experiences, all while driving commercial behaviors. To be eligible for winnings in the ICE Poker lounge, bettors must own and equip one of the ICE Poker NFT wearables. The poker games are free to play, but winners can earn $ICE tokens. When they're not playing poker, they can loan these wearables to other players, splitting the $ICE rewards if they win. With more than 16,000 NFT items and a floor price of around 2 ETH, they've built a solid community around this Web3 gambling experience.

We don't want to make it seem like Decentraland is fun only if you spend money. The vast majority of experiences in DCL revolve simply around participation. Games, events, and brand pop-ups are scattered all over DCL. What ties all of these disparate experiences together are POAPs, which stands for Proof-of-Acceptance Protocol. Many, but not all, of the experiences in DCL will gift visitors a POAP after they've attended the event or completed the game. You can think of POAPs as something like a Girl Scout Badge for achieving a new skill, your ticket stub from a concert, or a souvenir keychain from vacation. POAPs are digital mementos for showing that you're active in the Metaverse. Ultimately, POAPs are a reward mechanism and community-building tactic for bringing users into the Metaverse, without asking much of users in return. "Just come and have fun and we'll gift you a blockchain memento for joining us."

DappCraft, for example, built the SteamPunk Quest in Decentraland. It was a mini-game that asked players to fix their broken clock tower. Users had to scour their plot of land to find keys and solve puzzles in search of the seven gears needed to fix the clock. After completing the quest, users could claim their POAP. This was actually the first quest that we tried in Decentraland, and it was a fun way to spend 20 minutes. There are many games and events in DCL that offer POAPs, and they'll usually disclose on their https://events.decentraland.org page if they're offering up a POAP.

Other more recognizable brands have developed these POAP experiences as well. In anticipation of Super Bowl LVI, Miller Lite designed and launched the Meta Lite Bar in Decentraland. The Meta Lite Bar is a digital dive bar where patrons can pour a pilsner, play bar games, and get some free digital swag. The jukebox, pool table, darts, and bull-riding station are all interactive. It's Miller Lite's very own Metaverse destination, which we're sure they'll use for events in the future.

One of the more interesting aspects of the Meta Lite Bar is that it sits on a property that Miller Lite doesn't own. Rather, a company called TerraZero owns the DCL plot and rented the space to Miller, as well as helped them build out the bar. TerraZero offers up Metaverse land rentals so that agencies or individuals can test the waters before acquiring their own plot of land. Interestingly, TerraZero also initiated the first virtual home mortgage back in February 2022. The terms weren't disclosed; however, we do know that TerraZero holds the DCL property in their wallet until the loan is paid off. Virtual home mortgages could be an interesting means of accelerating Metaverse adoption, given that it opens up the pool of possible builders.

At this stage of the Metaverse, it's beneficial to simply have a presence in places like Decentraland. Whether or not there's a clear plan is beside the point. Simply being there is a strategy, a starting point that can allow them to deploy experiences whenever they see fit. For example, RE/MAX Turkey designed a virtual office in DCL. Sotheby's opened a digital replica of their New Bond Street headquarters in DCL and occasionally uses it to host live NFT auctions. Vice Media Group hired an actual architectural agency, BIG, to design their headquarters in DCL, which they plan to use either as a virtual news desk or innovation lab.

Brands and companies are establishing their presence in DCL in droves. Others are using the virtual world to extend their existing events. The Australian Open launched an entire venue in Decentraland during their tennis event. The digital venue hosted replays of the actual tennis matches, broadcasted 24/7 radio coverage, and featured a couple of tennis minigames.

The famed DJ that goes by 3LAU has the permanent 3LAU HAUS that is his own private music venue. He uses the space to host virtual concerts and reward his NFT collectors.

Decentraland is also no stranger to innovation. For example, Barbados is launching the world's first virtual embassy in the Metaverse, making them the first country to recognize digital sovereign land. They've teased the idea of issuing e-visas. What those will be used for, we have no clue. Regardless, this will be a great way for them to share their culture with the world and extend their diplomatic missions beyond their 18 current embassies. Who knows, they might just build out the industry for Metaverse tourism in the process.

Stepping away from the brands and institutional investments in DCL for a moment, we'd be remiss to not mention the independent DCL creators—folks who are entering this Metaverse, showcasing the experiences, and spreading the good word with the world.

The DCLBlogger (Matty) started creating informational Decentraland videos as far back as May 2018. His interest in Decentraland precedes these videos, as shown by his collection of some of the first wearables ever created in Decentraland. Matty's knowledge of DCL is rivaled by very few people. He's like an encyclopedia of everything that has gone down in DCL since its inception.

Another early DCL proponent goes by the name of SWISSVERSE. As far as we've seen, he's the first person to vlog their experiences in DCL using their Decentraland avatar as their front-facing vlogger. In many ways, SWISSVERSE's YouTube channel reminds us a lot of VTubers (short for "virtual YouTubers"). VTubers build their brand around an avatar that they animate using motion graphics software. The phenomenon dates back to the early 2010s in Japan but has since grown to an entire class of 10,000+ creators across YouTube, Twitch, Niconico, and Bilibili. SWISSVERSE is perhaps on a trend that could manifest into DCL influencers native to their platform.

Helping push this idea of DCL influencers into the forefront is the #DCLfilmclub. This community contest asks DCL residents to shoot a 30-second video showcasing their favorite aspects of Decentraland and submit their video on Twitter under the hashtag #DCLfilmclub. The top 10 video submissions (as voted on by their community) receive rewards in the form of $MANA tokens, wearables, and even a plot of LAND to first place—which was @TobikCC in 2022. With hundreds of submissions, contests like this show how dedicated the DCL user base is to share this platform with the world.

These cool showcases of the DCL community will always get overshadowed in the media by the hundred-thousand-dollar land sales. However, we believe the idea of DCL creators needs to be talked about more. It truly is a platform that enables storytelling on a limitless scale. In the same way that Instagram enabled a class of creators who specialize in social content, we believe that there will be a large class of Decentraland vloggers, musicians, photographers, and maybe even athletes.

If you're looking for a reason to believe in Decentraland, then we frankly have to tell you to buy into the long-term vision. It's an economy that will take time to build and manifest. If you compare it to the smooth operation of a *Roblox* or *Grand Theft Auto Online*, then you're already starting off on the wrong foot. A mobile interface and VR client are in the works. Voice chat and moderation software will improve. They're working on ways to integrate the number of profile-picture NFTs as a way to personalize your avatar. All of this and more are in the 2022 roadmap. Buy into the creators and investments being made in Decentraland, not just the way the media has portrayed them as a gold rush in digital land ownership.

The Sandbox

Behind Decentraland, The Sandbox is probably the most talked-about blockchain-based Metaverse. Interestingly, The Sandbox existed as an open-world sandbox game before they decided to add the blockchain element. The pre-blockchain version operates much like *Roblox*, offering tools for users to build their own worlds, assets, and games. However, to avoid covering anything redundant, we're going to skip over most of the pre-blockchain version of The Sandbox.

We will, however, say that there are two notable things they carry over from that era. One, The Sandbox was proficient at activating brand partnerships, and this is an area that has only accelerated as of late. Two, The Sandbox's developer, Pixowl, was acquired by Animoca Brands in 2018 for a little under $5 million USD. You might know Animoca from being a lead investor in Sky Mavis, the company behind Axie Infinity. This acquisition was significant because Animoca excels at blockchain gaming development, as showcased by two of their in-house projects: REVV Racing and F1 Delta.

The Sandbox will operate in many of the same ways as Decentraland, offering a scarce amount of ownable LAND to build on, an in-game utility and governance currency called $SAND, and a marketplace for accessories and assets. One of the areas that The Sandbox differentiates itself is its VoxEdit tool where users can create and animate voxel art. In other words, users can create in-game assets and upload them directly to their native NFT marketplace. Along the same lines, The Sandbox offers Game Maker, which is, as the name suggests, a tool in The Sandbox ecosystem where users can design their own games and deploy them on their LAND.

As of this writing (March 2022), The Sandbox only offers a download of their alpha version of the game for Windows (no Mac or mobile version yet). It's a fairly basic version of the game, but still affords you a sense of what will come.

Because The Sandbox is not yet live to the public, there's not a lot to talk about the platform that isn't speculative in nature. Therefore, it's pretty much a land grab in The Sandbox in preparation for what's to come. Still, there are a ton of notable brands, people, and players who have scooped up a significant amount of the 166,464 LANDs.

Household brands like Gucci, Adidas, Warner Music Group, and PwC Hong Kong have stakes in The Sandbox. The crypto exchanges Gemini, Binance, and FTX all own large properties. Gaming companies such Atari, Pong, Ubisoft, Yield Guild Games, and Chain Games are gearing up for their own gaming corners. After Snoop Dogg was touted for building his own mansion in The Sandbox, someone paid $450,000 USD for a LAND plot next door to be his digital neighbor.

We know that we're probably missing some key players who are aligning their interests in this Metaverse; however, we cannot possibly cover all of the people who own LAND in The Sandbox. If you're interested in exploring more of the LAND owners, just head to www.sandbox.game and click the "map" section. It displays images of who owns what LAND, and it's super fascinating to see just how many of your favorite entities are there.

Aside from LAND, there's been a decent amount of activity in their NFT marketplace as people prepare for the launch of the game. Hundreds of voxel artists are bringing their ideas to life in VoxEdit. Creators like TomGlasses, who is a toy designer, is building a variety of objects inspired by religion and mythology that people will be able to place on their LAND. The story that everyone loves to reference for its shock value is the MetaFlower Super Mega Yacht that sold for 149 ETH (or about $650,000 USD at the time of the sale). Ahead of the curve again, Snoop Dogg created and minted 10,000 unique Snoop-inspired avatars called The Doggies, which people can use as their own characters in the game.

Overall, The Sandbox has a long way to go before it surpasses the present utility and usability of Decentraland. Still, the platform has an aura surrounding it—a cool-factor element that seems to hover around its future.

Cryptovoxels

Another of the most-referenced sandbox Metaverses would be Cryptovoxels. Interestingly, its founder Ben Nolan worked on the Decentraland project for a short stint before deciding to build Cryptovoxels. This Metaverse offers the same features of both The Sandbox and Decentraland, so we won't reiterate those details around creator tools on the platform, a native currency $COLR, and the ability to own land and other assets there.

What stands out most to us regarding Cryptovoxels is that it's the only Metaverse that has found a clear product-market fit. The NFT and cryptoart movement has taken to Cryptovoxels as one of the de facto platforms for hosting NFT galleries. We believe this is because it's such a lightweight Metaverse that it doesn't require a lot of computing power to load, in addition to the fact that parcels are generally less expensive to acquire in Cryptovoxels. Regardless, they promote the use case of digital art galleries quite frequently. And given that NFT owners are more likely to also become Metaverse adopters, it's smart to position themselves in this manner.

Somnium Space

If you take Decentraland and add in a VR access point, then you get Somnium Space. Like the other sandbox Metaverses, Somnium Space is an open world built on the blockchain.

However, the fact that it's the first among these sandbox Metaverses to be able to be experienced in virtual reality is what stands out most.

Equally fascinating about Somnium Space is its plans to decentralize everything related to the Metaverse, even the hardware used to access it. Somnium Space has been working on a VR headset for some time now. Once it's released to the public, they plan on making it the first open source, modular headset. This means that headset owners can customize the look and feel of the device, which is particularly fascinating for anyone who has ideas on improving the design of VR headsets. We anticipate 3D printing enthusiasts eventually creating a market for these modular VR components—think straps, aesthetic cover plates, ergonomic handgrips, etc.

Many of the same events and experiences talked about in the other three sandbox Metaverses can also be found in Somnium Space. But one of the experiences unique to their platform, which we really liked, was a funding program that operates similar to *Shark Tank*. Whereas Decentraland has grant programs you can write proposals for, Somnium Space features a Creators Fund that asks virtual entrepreneurs to pitch their ideas in front of a panel of judges in their virtual studio, just like an episode of *Shark Tank*.

Honorable Mentions

The sandbox format for Metaverses is arguably the most interesting type of Metaverse out there given the freedom it offers its user base. However, it's also the most ambitious and difficult to pull off. This early on, it's tough to say for certain which one will win in the end, which is why so many Web3 enthusiasts are buying land in multiple sandbox Metaverse "just in case." For that reason, we feel it's necessary to shout out a few other sandbox Metaverses that might win the race to reach a critical mass of users.

Dvision Network is designing a hybrid of a gaming Metaverse and sandbox Metaverse, creating a lot of play-to-earn inroads to acquiring land in their open world. For those who cannot afford land outright, they've created a mechanism called LAND Purification. Forty percent of the LAND in Dvision is occupied by monsters that players must combat and clear (with their NFT characters). Once the LAND is cleared, it is put on the auction block whereby the final sale price in $DVI (their token) is distributed to the players, respective of their contributions to clearing the land. This is a unique concept for sandbox Metaverses, as it invites everyone no matter their financial standing to participate and earn in the game—eventually getting the opportunity to own property themselves.

NFT Worlds has combined their scarce land map with the ideology of a rarity scale associated with profile-picture NFTs. They offer 10,000 unique land assets with features such as formations (ocean, mountains, forests), natural resources (oil, gems, metals, freshwater), and rare features (towns, mineshafts, wild animals). The result is a sliding scale of rarity associated with each parcel of land, which is a concept we find truly fascinating in the grand scheme of Metaverse real estate.

Matrix World is building a virtual world on two blockchains: Flow and Ethereum. Multichain support is an interesting approach that we've seen other sandbox Metaverses tease. However, Matrix World was the first to mint and sell their land on both chains, half on Flow and half on Ethereum.

Genesis Worlds is taking a slightly different approach to designing the open-world Metaverse. Rather, we should say open worlds, plural. As opposed to creating a fixed map with a scarce amount of land, creators are invited to design an endless number of new worlds.

Substrata offers a unique take on the sandbox Metaverse, namely, that everything in their world doesn't have to exist as an NFT.

This 3D Metaverse gives users the power to design and deploy in-game assets, accessories, and objects on their land, but with the optionality to mint them as NFTs on Ethereum. In this sense, it is a bit of a hybrid between the former sandbox games like *Roblox* and the user-owned sandbox Metaverses we've discussed thus far.

Upland is another one of the early sandbox Metaverses to parlay the idea of owning and developing virtual real estate. Envisioned in 2018, Upland is interesting in that they designed their virtual map around the real world, featuring many of the major worldwide cities we know and love. In this sense, they're placing a sort of virtual mirror up to the real world and seeing how their Metaverse may grow alongside it.

At this point in time, it's tempting to go all-in on one sandbox Metaverse. But we implore you to check out the variety of sandbox Metaverses out there and keep an open mind. While they don't all necessarily offer something unique from their competitors, each of them is unique in their communities of users. So go browse their websites, follow their Twitter, and look for an upcoming event or experience that catches your interest. Enter the Sandbox Metaverse.

Gaming Metaverses

Often referred to as blockchain games, gaming Metaverses evolve the existing world of video games by offering truly ownable in-game assets and thus earning potential for players. Whereas games like *Fortnite* have pseudo-economies in their games, ultimately that money funnels up to the game's creators (Epic Games, in the case of *Fortnite*). But when you buy something like a weapon or wearable for your avatar in a gaming Metaverse, that money (minus a few fees, usually) goes to whoever owned and listed that asset on the marketplace.

Gaming Metaverses differ from sandbox Metaverses in that there is a clear goal for users in gaming Metaverses. Specifically, that goal is to progress in the game. Whether that progress is measured by leveling up characters, acquiring new items as NFTs, completing quests, or battling opponents, the goal in a gaming Metaverse is clear. And the more progress you make, the more you earn in the game.

Gaming Metaverses generally have their own currency that is used to incentivize gameplay and transact goods, in addition to governing the direction of the game. Underlying all gaming Metaverses' currencies are token economics (tokenomics), which dictate caps on the number of coins and deflationary token burning measures to ensure that their currency's value can appreciate as the game grows. Because these tokens are also traded on exchanges like Uniswap, PancakeSwap, and Sushiswap, and for some on Coinbase, there are many speculators who never play a blockchain game but still capitalize on their growth.

Axie Infinity is arguably the gaming Metaverse that jumpstarted this industry, as we discussed briefly in Chapter 4, "The History of the Metaverse." *Axie Infinity* proved that the model of play-to-earn economics could become really interesting once the game starts to scale. We won't go too much into how the game operates. But what's fascinating is that this game, which is valued at a few billion dollars now, inspired an entire ecosystem of development around the game. There are Twitch streamers, YouTube channels, and blogs dispersing strategies for being effective in the game. Players are forming guilds to team up and go further. Scholar programs have become a popular way to "rent out" one's own *Axie* characters to players throughout the world as a means of profit-sharing. The *Axie* ecosystem has grown far beyond the confines of the gaming platform and in the process inspired an entire wave of play-to-earn games in its wake.

We don't want to spend too much time digging into what makes each gaming Metaverse different, as their primary difference is usually their storytelling. In other words, the actual content of the game is what sets them apart and ultimately leads to some being more prominent than others. This doesn't mean that's the only way they differ. However, because the list of blockchain games goes on forever, we're going to let you explore what makes each of them different on your own time. With that being said, here are some of the notable gaming Metaverses (in alphabetical order) and a brief synopsis of them:

Aavegotchi is a Tamagotchi-inspired NFT collectible game that allows users to own NFT pets (Aavegotchis). Players can purchase and equip NFT assets to grow their Aavegotchis, which can ultimately explore and interact within the Aavegotchi gaming universe.

Alien Worlds consists of many explorable "exoPlanets" that users can own a stake in, vote on the development of, travel to using their NFT spacecraft, and mine for resources with NFT tools.

BigTime is an upcoming multiplayer role-playing game (RPG) where players team up and adventure through time and space together. In-game NFTs enable players to own and trade what they earn or buy in-game.

BYOVerse is building a gaming Metaverse starting with the NFT assets. Today, players can purchase BYOPills, which allow them to claim Apostles (characters) and then craft other NFT assets such as vehicles and accessories. This incentivizes their holders to essentially populate this Metaverse one asset at a time. Also, the team has partnered with other games such as Galaxy Fight Club, making BYOPills an interoperable gaming NFT with utility across games.

Cradles is a "prehistoric Metaverse" game that mirrors real-world time and space rules starting in the Triassic Age of dinosaurs. Players collect items to advance time and explore the different eras of life on Earth.

CryptoTanks is a play-to-earn tank battling game inspired by the 1090s Nintendo game *Battle City*. The goal is to level up one's NFT CryptoTank and earn $TANK tokens in the process. Players can also rent their tank to other players when they're not active in order to earn profit-share.

DeHorizon is building an immersive gaming Metaverse around three distinct experiences, team battles, battle royale tournaments, and dragon racing. Their team has extensive game development backgrounds from Riot, Dungeons & Dragons, and Blizzard.

Ember Sword is a free-to-play MMORPG that allows players to acquire land and collectibles that help them progress in player-versus-player gameplay.

Enjin aims to build a unified Metaverse gaming platform that developers can use to build and deploy games swiftly. Their premise is that by unifying multiple games under the same token, they can create a gaming ecosystem that helps all games grow and reach a critical mass of players.

F1 Delta Time is a blockchain game that centers around the collection and trading of unique NFT cars, drivers, and components—ultimately with the goal of winning races and prizes. It's the official blockchain game of F1 racing.

Illuvium is a collectible NFT RPG game and auto-battler rolled into one. There is an open-world RPG experience in the Overworld, where players mine, harvest, capture, and fight Illuvials. Once players have assembled a team, they can join the auto-battler where players strategically build their teams to beat opponents in battle.

Legacy is a blockchain-based business simulator game where players can start and grow businesses. It's a game that is supposed to emulate the free market, with the most creative and value, providing players benefits from higher volumes of trade and transactions.

Mirandus is a fantasy world gaming Metaverse created by Gala Games. The MMORPG allows players to create the content they desire, with five different avatar types that offer different abilities in the game.

My Neighbor Alice is a multiplayer building game where players buy and own virtual islands while collecting and building items and connecting with new friends. The farm-themed world is inspired by *Animal Crossing* and offers NFTs as in-game assets. Users can play-to-earn the $ALICE token, which can then be used to purchase items, stake for rewards, and governance.

OneRare is a gaming Metaverse celebrating food in Web3. Players can farm ingredient NFTs, sell their produce at the market, create NFT dishes in the kitchen, and battle against friends in mini-games. It's meant to be the culinary industry's entry point into Web3, offering food brands, chefs, and restaurants a means to build in the Metaverse.

Star Atlas is a grand strategy game of space exploration, territorial conquest, political domination, and more. Players compete to explore new planets, outfitting their spacecraft and avatars to conquer lands ahead of rival factions.

Wilder World is creating an open, mixed-reality Metaverse themed around a "1980s Miami meets cyberpunk." Wilder World is building a virtual city, called Wiami, where creators can manifest their ideas, players can equip different NFT accessories, and this open source world can grow organically.

They've partnered with Zer0 on the tech side to offer a blended-reality experience, whereby NFT assets can be transported to real-life locations to be viewed through the Zer0 Augmented Reality App.

Most of these gaming Metaverses do not offer a Metaverse-like experience where you're actually exploring a 3D world. They are mostly experienced through 2D interfaces, with many of them yet to be fully developed. Still, they all have plans of rolling out 3D worlds of their own or integrating with some of the sandbox Metaverses discussed earlier in this chapter.

As far as immersive Metaverse games go, the clear front-runner here would have to be the entire Oculus VR platform. We know that it doesn't show any signs of enabling blockchain integrations; however, when it comes to Metaverse gaming, it's hard to argue with the beautiful games built here. Games like *The Walking Dead: Saints & Sinners*, *Superhot VR*, *Demeo*, and *Pistol Whip* are all really impressive. We would argue that the Oculus VR headset is really a gaming platform, which Meta would probably agree with considering they put the *Beat Saber* game front and center in advertisements. Of course, before there was Oculus gaming, we had PS VR. PlayStation's take on virtual reality gaming introduced a lot of people to this concept of immersive gaming. The next evolution is adding blockchain to the fold.

Overall, gaming Metaverses are by far the most competitive landscape, but also the one wrought with the most ambitious plans that will likely never materialize. Designing and deploying games is not something that can normally be achieved in months, let alone years. So we argue that you should take each of these gaming Metaverses with a grain of salt before getting too invested in them.

Miscellaneous Metaverses

Not every Metaverse company wants to create an explorable, virtual world akin to the one imagined in *Snow Crash* or *Ready, Player One*. There are many companies solving problems that will enhance the overall experience of the Metaverse. They are what we like to call Metaverse-adjacent companies.

These Metaverse-adjacent companies are solving for things like realistic digital presence, commerce portals that connect to the physical world, readymade Metaverse environments that anyone can plug into, and the social experience of the Metaverse.

Digital Presence

While most of the Metaverse experiences are created in a sort of cartoonish or video-game style, there's a camp of people who believe that the Metaverse should look as realistic as possible.

Wolf Digital World, for example, has created a full-body scanner that can scan objects into a digital format in 16k graphics. They call it the metascanner, and they market it as a tool for helping people license their likeness, their creations, and their assets in the Metaverse. Naturally, they've already partnered with a Metaverse company (Metahero) to have a virtual space where these scans live. Overall, it gives new meaning to a personalized avatar—one that is literally you in a digital format. But this also has implications for assets like sculptures, high-end furniture, and even automobiles. Brands who want a digital twin of their creations have an easy on-ramp into the Metaverse with the metascanner.

Similarly, Matterport offers the same service except targeted at physical spaces. To date, they've scanned and generated digital replicas of more than 5 million spaces. Although the majority of their clients have been in real estate, their tech has seen a boom in architecture and engineer planning use cases, retail inventory management, and even assessing risk for insurance policies. Matterport is the perfect example of a Metaverse-adjacent company since its tech isn't designed for the Metaverse, but can surely be applied to this vision.

For those who are looking for an easier option, Apple's Object Capture can also be used to quickly create high-fidelity virtual objects by only using an iPhone.

All of this tech will help populate realistic environments in the Metaverse. In some cases, a realistic digital presence may be preferred, and thus these three technologies could facilitate that.

Phygital Commerce

Naturally, every brand that is eyeing the Metaverse is curious about how they can serve this new market of consumers. But not every brand is either equipped or interested in selling NFTs. That doesn't mean they cannot participate here. However, they may be more inclined to sell existing physical products, rather than new digital products, in the Metaverse.

Commerce in the Metaverse is still coming of age. Furthermore, it is difficult to estimate when shopping for real-world goods in the Metaverse will become mainstream. But solving at least the technical side of this unknown are two notable companies.

Earlier in the "Decentraland" section, we talked about a company called Boson Protocol that is creating a means for Metaverse shoppers to purchase physical goods and have them delivered to their actual front doorstep. Their protocol solves some of the ambiguity around identifying people in the Metaverse, which is easier said than done. The experiences that they create through their Boson Portals (the actual customizable storefronts) are a hybrid of NFT buying and e-commerce shopping.

Boson's competition in this space is a company called Highstreet. Highstreet is planning to create a sort of sandbox Metaverse with physical and digital retail embedded alongside one another. Their Metaverse shopping experience will deliver "phygital" goods, which are essentially goods that users will own both as physical products and digital NFT assets. Similar to the sandbox Metaverses, Highstreet has already had a land sale or Initial Home Offering, as they called it. And those with land in Highstreet can use the Metaplex Merchant Portal to create virtual storefronts for this phygital shopping.

Most of us live a significant portion of our life online, so it makes sense that companies want to use the Metaverse as a new e-commerce experience. How Metaverse shopping ultimately plays out is still to be determined.

Readymade Metaverse Environments

Not everyone who is interested in the Metaverse wants to take the time to design their own space. For this challenge, readymade Metaverse environments offer up a unique way for individuals or brands to plug right in and offer their own Metaverse experience nearly instantly.

Spatial is the leader in providing readymade Metaverse environments. They started as a VR communications company that was designed as a sort of social Metaverse space. But when the NFT boom happened in 2021, they quickly found that the vast majority of their new users were using Spatial as a place to host NFT galleries. Spatial quickly pivoted and began offering Metaverse design services. For example, they helped create the Utah Jazz's virtual locker room in partnership with Krista Kim (known for the Mars House) and Michael Potts (CEO of M2 Studios). Today, they design readymade Metaverse galleries and Metaverse environments, minting a scarce quantity of them as NFTs. For example, coauthor QuHarrison purchased five of their Museo NFTs, which are predesigned NFT galleries that you can populate with your NFTs.

Another company called Space Metaverse recently raised $7 million USD to offer a similar experience. Although they want to be more of a "Shopify for the Metaverse," offering some of those phygital shopping experiences we just mentioned, they start brands off with premade Metaverse environments to plug into.

Because access to quality 3D designers is so scarce and in demand right now, we see a huge opportunity for individuals and companies to offer readymade Metaverses to corporations, particularly the Fortune 500.

Social VR Worlds

Ultimately, the Metaverse isn't going to work without a significant user base. This entire book (and Meta's future) is moot if the Metaverse is not appealing to people. For this reason, you need on-ramps into these Metaverse experiences. Two VR apps that have done a wonderful job onboarding people into virtual worlds are VRChat and Bigscreen.

VRChat is a low-friction app for people to design virtual spaces and host social gatherings. Since 2014, its user base has created more than 25,000 virtual worlds to inhabit and socialize in. Interestingly, a lot of subcultures such as Anime enthusiasts have been the power users here. However, Meta's vision of Horizon Worlds being the home to social experiences was already proven by VRChat. And there's even one user by the name of Joe Hunting who filmed a documentary about VRChat, called *We Met in Virtual Reality*, that is shot entirely in VRChat. The film chronicles stories of what makes VRChat (and therefore the Metaverse) so compelling from a social connection standpoint and, fingers crossed, will hopefully be accepted into one of the major film festivals in 2022.

Bigscreen is another one of the low-friction VR worlds that has seen early success as a virtual social hangout. What's cool about Bigscreen is that their product allows users to simultaneously watch movies and play games together, while in the same virtual room. It's like the equivalent of that one childhood friend who had the coolest basement that everyone hung out in. Except now, it's a virtual basement.

The Mass Migration to the Metaverse

The one question that persists in the back of every Metaverse-builder's mind is "How do we get users into the Metaverse?" While we'd like to think that there will be something along the lines of an "iPhone moment" where a Steve-Jobs-type parlays this ideal vision of the Metaverse and everyone feels the need to get involved, this sadly won't be the case.

The mass migration to the Metaverse won't be a mass migration at all. It's going to be a bunch of small, incongruent moments of people making their way to the Metaverse. *Axie Infinity* and the gaming Metaverses are doing their best to bring the billion-plus gamers over to the Metaverse. Decentraland and the sandbox Metaverses are doing their best to bring the capitalists, the builders, and the opportunists to the Metaverse. And of course, Meta is using their Oculus VR hardware as an entry point to introduce millions to the wonders of VR.

People would like to believe that there will be one experience that turns the Metaverse from an area of interest into a habitual need, in the same way that the news feed turned social media from something you check every once in a while into an addictive habit. But truthfully, the Metaverse is simply too vast an idea to entice people with one experience.

We say all that to say that the mass migration to the Metaverse will happen slowly over time. People need to see that there's a Metaverse experience out there that aligns with an interest they already have. The day that you can watch, or rather experience, every single NBA game in the Metaverse is the day that NBA fans will begin making their way over to the Metaverse and building their basketball fan communities. The day that it is easy for Pinterest board creators to monetize their mood boards in the Metaverse is the day that these hobbyists will venture over to the Metaverse.

We change our digital habits when it is convenient for us— when an interest of ours shows up somewhere else and improves upon the existing way to experience that interest. Furthermore, we change when our friends change.

Fortunately, the growth of any one of the sandbox, gaming, or miscellaneous Metaverses is growth for the entire industry. People need to familiarize themselves with the idea of virtual existence. And no matter where that takes place, once people are familiar with it, they are more likely to explore other Metaverses.

As a professional looking for opportunities at your business, as a creative looking for new ways to build, or simply as an individual looking for the next way to socially connect, it's important that you stay nimble and try the variety of Metaverses out there. Don't lock yourself into one destination, and definitely don't lock yourself into one idea of what the Metaverse will ultimately be. After all, at a time when the Metaverse is still to be defined, it's too early to be operating in definites.

7

Metaverse Assets

As far back as the mid-1990s, people have been caring for digital pets. Tamagotchi envisioned that humans could have a personal connection with an artificial being on a screen. It's a bizarre concept when you say that people will care for a digital file. But when you make that digital file a cute avatar, make that digital file's survival rely on your routine check-ins, and then put them on a handy keychain, you've crafted the perfect storm for people having a connection with a digital asset. Tamagotchis became so popular throughout the late 1990s and early 2000s that schools nationwide had to ban these devices because they were so distracting. Students were sneaking them around school because they couldn't be away from their Tamagotchi for too long. If that's not the ideal reason to justify the current NFT craze, then we don't know what is.

After Tamagotchi, Internet versions like *Neopets* and *Webkinz* took their place. The Internet allowed for much more functionality and immersion with one's digital pet. And then with handheld devices came *Nintendogs* and later *Animal Crossing*, which showed us just how large the digital pet industry was. Currently, *Animal Crossing: New Horizons* is 13th on the list of best-selling video games of all time, with a total of more than 37 million copies sold worldwide. And the game was only recently launched in March 2020.

Digital pets laid the groundwork for people caring about digital assets (and thus, Metaverse assets). It's odd to call a pet an asset. We apologize to all of the animal lovers out there. We know this sounds crass. But it's kind of the truth. After all, don't we call ourselves "pet owners" in the same way we refer to ourselves as homeowners?

The point we're making here is that our assets are a large part of who we are for three reasons:

- **Our assets reflect our identity:** We buy stuff that represents who we are or who we want to become. The clothes you wear show the personality you embody. The way you furnish your house reflects what type of environment best suits you.

- **Our assets reflect our community:** We buy things to show what tribe we are a part of or want to be a part of. Millions of people stop by Starbucks every morning because holding a Starbucks cup means something; it means you're part of the Starbucks coffee community.

- **Our assets reflect our status:** We purchase certain brands because they signal status in society. From the watch you wear to the car you drive to the purse you hold, these things show what class you are in. With assets that signal status also comes scarcity and therefore the additional opportunity for financial incentives.

These three factors play a large part in understanding Metaverse assets and why they make sense in the grand scheme of our lives.

To round out our argument, let's go back to digital pets. This industry hasn't stopped with *Animal Crossing*. In fact, it has now evolved with the introduction of NFTs, imbuing a true sense of ownership of one's digital pet.

For example, Genopets are an NFT-based digital pet game with large Metaverse-related ambitions. The entire experience revolves around creating a digital pet that mirrors who you are. It starts with a personality quiz, which ensures that your *identity* is matched with the right Genopet. By owning a Genopet, you show that you're part of the greater *community* of digital pet lovers. And as you progress throughout the game, your Genopet levels up in a way that signals your *status* as a digital pet owner. Genopets reflect the trinity of reasons why we own the assets we own.

Now, Genopets are much more than this. The game is proving the model of Move-to-Earn economics—an offshoot of play-to-earn whereby progress and earning in the game rely on one's activity levels. To achieve this, Genopets is the first NFT-based project to integrate with Apple Health and Google Fit. But simply as a Metaverse asset, Genopets are a great metaphor for understanding this market for NFTs and Metaverse assets.

In general, we relate people's fondness for NFTs to the way that people are fond of their pets. We all know at least a couple of people who love their dog or cat more than they love most of their friends. In the theoretical situation where someone offered these pet owners 10 times the amount of money for their pet than they paid for it, they'd scoff and say no. Now, there's a price for everything, and we're sure at a certain point they'd consider the offer. But those figures would have to be quite lofty. The same goes for NFT owners.

We know people who won't part ways with an NFT that is worth north of $100,000 USD because they think the image is cute. How can one possibly care for a digital file that much where they won't take a 10x or sometimes 100x return on their investment? It's a hard concept to wrap your head around. But it's a behavior that is more common than you think.

If we dig deeper, though, the real explanation for why people won't part with their NFTs is that trinity of reasons we identified before: identity, community, and status. And that's what Metaverse assets are all about. We connect with our digital assets in the same way we connect with our physical assets. People care for their NFTs similarly to how they care for their pets.

Furthermore, digital escapism is real. We use digital destinations to ease the pains of daily life. When work grinds us down, we pull out our phones and play a quick game of *Candy Crush* to get that jolt of accomplishment. When our lives seem boring and uneventful, we turn to Instagram and Tik Tok to live vicariously through others. And for the many who struggle to make friends in the "real" world, *Fortnite* and *NBA 2k* are always there to help us form digital friendships.

As we argue throughout this entire book, the Metaverse is gearing up to be the next great digital escape. And for the first time, everyone can now own pieces of their digital escapes because of blockchain and NFTs. Except for maybe monks, we all take digital escapes on a daily basis. Therefore, the opportunity to own and potentially profit from your digital escape should be welcomed by all.

With that being said, what exactly are people buying in preparation for the Metaverse? What Metaverse assets can we, or will we, own?

What We Will Own in the Metaverse

There are many digital creators testing the waters with what types of NFTs people will connect with today. The NFT market runs largely in parallel to Metaverse assets. However, it's not a 1:1 match, per se. In other words, every NFT will not be a Metaverse asset, just like every Metaverse asset does not necessarily have to be an NFT.

But we can look at the NFT market to extract insight into the types of assets we may own and use in the Metaverse. We can use the phenomenon of NFTs, this market that sold more than $20 billion USD worth of digital files in 2021, to envision how we may populate the Metaverse with user-owned goods.

When we look at digital presence and the concept of digital ownership in the Metaverse, we can organize these assets around four categories: avatars, accessories, objects, and real estate. At the smallest unit of digital presence is the avatar—the manifestation of people in the Metaverse. Accessories are what the avatar equips, adding layers of personality to our digital presence. Objects and things are what the avatar owns in order to color in their experiences in the Metaverse but cannot equip on their person. Finally, the largest unit of digital presence is real estate, the land and buildings an avatar can call their property and thus their space to contribute to the Metaverse's experience.

In the following subsections, we're going to jump between Metaverse assets that exist today and theoretical assets that we feel will be created and owned in the Metaverse. Every single one of these Metaverse assets relates to the trinity of reasons we choose to buy the assets we buy: identity, community, and status. As we flow through these examples of Metaverse assets, think about which of the three reasons is embedded in that particular use case of digital ownership.

Avatars

You can be whoever you want to be in the Metaverse. That's one of the underlying promises of this limitless new world. Whether you want to appear as a giant sloth, take the figure of an anthropomorphic water bottle, or look as you do in reality, that's your prerogative. Zuckerberg drove this point home in their announcement of Meta as he gathered around a virtual card table with one guy who looked "normal," one woman that chose to be a flickering hologram, a third person that was floating as if in space, and another character that took the form of a robot.

Although most of the Metaverses discussed in Chapter 6, "Enter the Metaverse," don't quite afford us this level of creative freedom, this is the direction that avatars are ultimately headed. The avatar you choose to materialize in the Metaverse is your choice to make.

When we look at the current NFT market, the projects that signal what we're likely to experience as avatars in the Metaverse are none other than the PFP projects (PFP is short for profile picture). For example, CryptoPunks, Bored Apes, Cool Cats, Gutter Cats, and World of Women are all considered PFP NFTs. These collections generally consist of anywhere between 3,000 and 10,000 unique NFT characters that feature a variety of traits (different hair colors, facial accessories like piercings, outfits, etc.).

The reason that PFP NFTs will likely take shape as avatars in the Metaverse is that PFPs have been instrumental in forming digital communities. Every PFP project has a Discord chat group that allows only those holders access. Owners of said PFPs take enormous pride in being one of the 10,000 holders, oftentimes changing their Twitter profile pictures to these NFT characters. When Twitter unveiled a verification feature that allowed people with NFT profile pictures to prove that they owned said NFTs, it solidified this concept of communities forming around PFPs.

Community is important in the Metaverse just as it is important here in the physical world. And PFPs will help contribute to building community in the Metaverse.

But how do these 2D JPEGs become 3D avatars?

We love referencing two particular projects to color in this transition. One of the projects is called Cryptopunk is Alive. Basically, they took the existing CryptoPunks collection and re-created their appearance on real human models. They applied makeup, groomed facial hair, donned hats, and literally made these 2D NFTs into 3D people. Now, this is a manual process and likely won't be how Metaverse avatars take shape as PFP NFTs. But it shows what that transition from 2D to 3D looks like and what changes in the process.

Our second example that shows how 2D JPEGs transition to 3D avatars is a project called MetaSports Basketball. It's a block-chain game where players can upload their PFP NFTs and have them populate as 3D avatars in their basketball game. Every so often, they make an announcement on Twitter that they support a new PFP project. One by one, they integrate the PFP world with their game. And each announcement acts as a marketing play to bring new users into their game.

The PFP project that really understood how NFTs might one day be our avatars in the Metaverse was Meebits. Created by Larva Labs (the team behind CryptoPunks), Meebits are just like other PFP NFTs except that owners are also given access to a 3D file of their Meebit in the .vox format. Because Metaverses like The Sandbox and Cryptovoxels are largely built in the .vox file format, there will come a day when Meebits owners can bring their NFT characters into these virtual worlds.

Today, when you enter Decentraland or The Sandbox or Meta Horizons, you can build your avatar from their list of possible characteristics. While there haven't been any announcements from these platforms that they will integrate with PFP NFTs at large, we believe it is inevitable because it's a feature that will give purpose to NFT collectors becoming Metaverse users. Logistically, they'll need to design a tool that can autopopulate a PFP into their platform's format. It's possible that a third party may create this technology, but it's more likely that they'll create this tool in-house to fit the specs of their platform.

Equally important to your avatar, though, is the name that you give it. This applies mostly to the blockchain-based Metaverses where names are scarce and ownable assets just like land. In Decentraland, you can buy names starting at around 100 MANA. There's an entire subgroup of speculators who are snapping up plausibly valuable names like Satoshi (creator of Bitcoin), Versace, and Bank in hopes that they can flip them on the secondary marketplace for a profit. For example, one user minted the name KanyeWest on the blockchain two years ago and recently resold it for 100,000 MANA (which is equivalent to ~$260,000 USD). Because plots of land can also take on these unique names, names of landmarks and businesses have been among the most speculated DCL names, as well as the most successfully resold name assets.

More general to the entire NFT market is the Ethereum Name Service (ENS). The ENS provides a standard for creating and owning blockchain names and domains. They work as a naming registry for simplifying one's blockchain wallet address. If you have a blockchain wallet, then you know that it is virtually impossible to memorize your 42-character wallet address. However, you can buy an ENS name, which is formatted with a suffix of `.eth`, and then program that ENS name to relay funds to your blockchain wallet. Today, your ENS domain can be used to simplify your wallet address, direct people to a website, and do a few other things. But there's a future where these ENS domains will also be the standard for our usernames in the Metaverse, thus financializing another important part of digital presence into an ownable Metaverse asset.

That about sums up avatars and avatar names. Now, let's move onto the Metaverse assets that our avatars will equip.

Accessories

Half of the fun of existing as a digital avatar is accessorizing that avatar. To our point about assets playing a role in our identity, Metaverse accessories will help us express ourselves to the fullest. When it comes to accessories, we're talking about anything that your avatar can wear or equip on their person. We're making this clear distinction to not mix them up with the following section on Metaverse objects.

To relay this idea of Metaverse accessories, a lot of people will turn to existing markets like *Fortnite*'s Item Shop for backpacks, gliders, and even dance emotes. These digital goods in *Fortnite* don't directly impact gameplay, but they're a great means of personal expression and style in the game. For example, players can add the "Sap" wrap to their weapons in order to make it appear as though they're using a wooden gun. Although this wrap and the thousands of skins out there aren't going to boost your gun's damage, they signal status in *Fortnite*. And nobody wants to play in stock equipment. *Fortnite* accessories and the entire industry for in-game consumer spending is a massive business, representing more than $54 billion USD in 2020 and an estimated $65 billion USD in 2022.

This is why so many brands and designers are excited about the Metaverse accessories market, with some already getting a leg up on this new asset class.

Metaverse accessories at their core are for style and expression. If you go to https://market.decentraland.org, you'll find tens of thousands of different accessories ranging in price from less than a dollar to a few thousand dollars. People are selling everything from T-shirts and sunglasses to wings and energy auras. The vast majority of these wearables don't change what you can do in Decentraland. However, this budding market for in-game accessories already accounts for nearly $120 million USD in Decentraland sales, according to DappRadar (this figure also includes land and names).

Digital fashion, in general, has been quite hyped as it relates to the Metaverse. We've seen fashion brands from Versace to Gucci create digital outfits and sell them as NFTs. Coca-Cola dropped a 1/1 NFT collection that came with a Coke-branded digital puffer coat. The Fabricant is a fashion studio that specializes in creating digital clothing in its most impressive and imaginative form. And teams like RTFKT have risen to the top of the digital fashion industry with their periodic digital sneaker drops (before Nike acquired them). Although none of the aforementioned fashion wearables can be ported into existing Metaverse platforms, it shows that there is interest for valuable and scarce digital clothing.

Ultimately, the vision is for Metaverse accessories to have utility. We're drawn to the example set by a team called Jadu. They've released a collection of Jadu Jetpacks and Jadu Hoverboards that will be able to be used for transportation in The Sandbox once the game is launched. They've taken to a similar NFT collection format as the PFP projects, releasing 7,777 of their voxel transportation devices, each imbued with different characteristics and rarity levels.

Outside of transportation as a utility, Metaverse accessories can also work as access keys. We mentioned the ICE Poker wearables in Chapter 6. These NFT accessories, once equipped on one's avatar in Decentraland, allow players to enter the ICE Poker lounge where they can compete in poker tournaments for prizes. As far as utility for Metaverse accessories goes, we feel that "access" will be one of the most widespread forms of utility that they will provide.

So many NFT project creators have used funds from their sales to purchase land in the Metaverse, which they plan to build out as community headquarters. For example, The MetaKey owns large plots in both Decentraland and The Sandbox. The MetaKey's creator, DCLBlogger, plans to make these destinations exclusive to MetaKey holders, providing all sorts of events and experiences for his community to enjoy. As we mentioned in Chapter 6, 3LAU created the 3LAU HAUS in Decentraland, which is a concert venue for his NFT holders.

Earlier in the "Avatars" section, we talked about how PFP projects may one day take shape as avatars, but we also feel that the Metaverse at large will be instrumental in providing an "in-person" value to holders of certain NFT projects. We look at a project like Dirt, which was the world's first newsletter funded by NFT sales. That team, which is led by Kyle Chayka and Daisy Alioto, is building out the Dirtyverse—an entire ecosystem of media-related events for their supporters. Today, those events and experiences are delivered in the traditional Web2 formats via Zoom hangouts and emails. But they've already expressed ideas for how they might design a space around their mascot, Dirt, which will be exclusive to their NFT holders.

Ultimately, Metaverse accessories are as limitless as the mind can imagine. In their most basic form, they are assets for expressing our identity and status. But what they really create is a community around a shared style or interest and thus contribute to forming our unique identities. The future utility that Metaverse accessories provide is everything from boosting gameplay abilities to providing access to gated experiences. This type of Metaverse asset may seem strange and a waste of money today. But as the userbases of the Metaverse grow, we'll see Metaverse accessories take on a similar importance in digital presence as Rolexes, Christian Louboutin red-bottom heels, and VIP passes do in our physical presence.

Objects

Everything that isn't either virtual real estate or an accessory for your avatar we are classifying as Metaverse objects. Obviously, this can include objects such as yachts, art, or furniture for your home, but it also extends much further. The term *objects* is more a catchall for the "category-less" Metaverse assets. In that sense, it's the most expansive category and also the one that requires you to put on your futurist cap to envision the possibilities.

First, we'd classify digital pets as Metaverse objects. We could see Genopets following us around in the Metaverse one day, being our digital sidekicks that visualize how healthy we are in the real world. ClassicDoge is another team working on the idea of "NFT-ing" digital pets. What's cool about their project is that you can submit pictures of your actual dog and they'll create a digital edition of it. In this sense, they're providing a means to memorialize your pet in the Metaverse, which has major implications for all the dog lovers out there.

Another interesting Metaverse object is the MetaPortal by MetaMundo. The MetaPortal is a sort of alien technology that can transport owners to special locations in the Metaverse. It can be placed anywhere within one's digital real estate. And they plan to collaborate with all sorts of other Metaverse creators to create exclusive destinations in the Metaverse that only the MetaPortal can teleport people to.

There's a vision of the future where we actually own gaming consoles in the Metaverse. The founder of Vine, Dom Hofmann, has been working on a project called Supdrive for some time. Supdrive will be a digital NFT-based gaming console where people can own scarce copies of video games, which are represented as NFTs. Along the same lines, we could see the arcades of the past being reimagined in the Metaverse. Atari or Stern Pinball might one day design digital replicas of their iconic arcade games, allowing people to place a pinball machine or *Pac-Man* in their Metaverse home. Furthermore, there are already discussions around creating Metaverse arcades featuring classic games, outfitting one's property with virtual arcade machines that charge a small amount of digital currency to play.

Any object that we fill our homes, offices, and spaces with will have a market in the Metaverse. From furniture and picture frames to appliances and tools, all of these objects can and will exist as Metaverse objects. It takes a little bit of imagination to envision how they can bring utility to the greater Metaverse experiences. And it definitely requires design and marketing prowess to make people want them. But the more you think about the Metaverse as people's second homes, the more you'll come to understand why we will need to fill these homes with objects that provide utility, invoke memories, or help us experience the Metaverse to the fullest.

Speaking of the Metaverse as our "home away from home," we arrive at the reason many have come to hear about the Metaverse: virtual real estate.

Real Estate

If you've read any articles or watched news segments that talk about the virtual land rush, then you've probably heard virtual real estate compared to the idea of buying real estate in Manhattan in the 1700s. It's an analogy that has circulated far and wide, propagating the idea that virtual real estate returns will realize massive, no, astronomical returns.

But this analogy glosses over two major assumptions. One is that this return will be realized in this lifetime. What's the time horizon on this investment after all? Two is that you cannot lose no matter what plot of virtual real estate you purchase. Where should you purchase virtual land?

In reality, picking virtual real estate today (if we use the 1700s analogy) would be like looking at a map of North America and saying, "Pick any 100sq mile plot and call it yours." With the variety of Metaverses and the large quantity of land in each, this is a more realistic analogy of what it feels like to invest in virtual real estate today.

Granted, there are some Metaverses whose virtual real estate seems to be more of a sure bet than others. Given that Decentraland and The Sandbox have garnered the most interest, we'd be more inclined to invest in their real estate. Still, it's a major risk that relies on the overall success of the Metaverse.

Furthermore, how do you pick the right plot of land? After all, we don't truly know what land will appreciate the most. With more than 90,000 plots in Decentraland and more than 165,000 plots in The Sandbox, it feels kind of like a guessing game.

Some Metaverse land investors employ the strategy of predicting what plots will see the most foot traffic and thus the most marketability to Metaverse businesses. This might result in picking plots near public points of interests or right next to major roads and thoroughfares.

Others have adopted a strategy of mirroring where the financial whales and major players in the NFT space are staking their territory. For example, the person who purchased a plot next door to Snoop Dogg in The Sandbox was clearly using this strategy. Pranksy is seen as an NFT whale and owns a substantial plot in The Sandbox, as well. Plots surrounding Pranksy's might become more valuable. This strategy goes for mirroring corporate investments as well, buying land near Atari, Adidas, or Samsung. Naturally, once these businesses build an experience in the Metaverse, they are likely to see a lot of foot traffic, and therefore the surrounding plots are bound to receive the spillage.

If you're looking to buy your first plot of Metaverse land but are struggling with the optionality, Parcel provides a nice interface for seeing every piece of virtual real estate on the market. Positioning themselves as the Zillow for Metaverse Land, Parcel aggregates all of the virtual land on the market from Decentraland, The Sandbox, Somnium Space, and Cryptovoxels, making it simpler to compare prices and options across the most popular Metaverse landscapes.

While the vast majority of virtual real estate owners have yet to develop their properties in a significant way, this is the next step for advancing the Metaverse. In Chapter 6, we discussed the idea of readymade Metaverse environments that Spatial was creating. This idea will be applied to the Metaverse in the form of readymade architecture. Essentially, creators will design and build architecture for a specific Metaverse and sell them on the open market—giving people a plug-and-play option for developing their land in a low-effort way. We look at a project like The Meeting Place, which was a readymade Metaverse environment created by Benny Or and Cyril Lancelin. The Meeting Place can be plugged into a variety of virtual worlds (none of the blockchain Metaverses yet) and utilized as a meeting ground for designers and other professionals.

Ultimately, architecture matters in the Metaverse. We bring up The Meeting Place because it is so beautifully designed and helps show just what's possible in the gravity-free Metaverse. There will be an entire class of Metaverse architects who specialize in helping people build on their property. We've already seen it take shape with the organization Voxel Architects, which has been contracted by a few Metaverse landowners to build on their properties.

Owning real estate in the Metaverse is cool, but developing that land into something that others can experience and enjoy is the true manifestation of Metaverse real estate.

Metaverse Asset Management

NFTs introduced the world to a new asset class that can appreciate at a rate only rivaled by cryptocurrency. Many first-time millionaires have been made in just months, bringing a flood of excitement to digital assets. Of course, this market is not devoid of bad actors. However, the transparency that the blockchain provides to this emerging asset class has kept these bad actors at bay thanks to what we like to call *blockchain investigators*.

Blockchain investigators scour transaction histories on Etherscan to build cases against those who are taking advantage of NFTs and NFT investors. We saw this first play out when blockchain investigators were able to deduce that the Fame Lady Squad NFT project, which was marketed as the first women-led PFP NFT project, was in fact led by three men. The NFT community rallied behind this controversy and ultimately dethroned these leaders, replacing them with women who were Fame Lady holders.

More recently, an NFT industry watchdog that goes by the Twitter handle @NFTethics built a case around one of the more

respected NFT players by the name of @beaniemaxi. NFTethics'
report detailed numerous occasions where Beanie used his influence to deceive his followers in pump-and-dump scams that he
held positions in, didn't disclose, and then siphoned his funds out
before the projects shuttered. For over a week, Beanie's figura-
tive beheading took place across NFT Twitter circles until he
was essentially blacklisted from every NFT community, project,
as well as his own GM Capital VC fund.

The blockchain, in theory, will help eradicate some of the
foul play and incestuous financial practices that take place in free
markets. By now, we've seen this eradication happen many times
over. While many are still slipping through the cracks, the swift-
ness with which we've seen some of this foul play in the NFT
market stamped out is encouraging for anyone looking to invest
in Metaverse assets.

We cannot deny that the market for digital assets at large is
extremely volatile, totally unpredictable, and at times downright
frightening to anyone involved. This ultimately has made many
potential investors avoid this new market. But the unpredictabil-
ity is a result of not being engaged with the NFT community,
having conversations with other collectors, tuning into Twitter
Spaces, and just understanding where the digital assets with an
actual chance at longevity lie.

We realize that throughout this book we've exposed you to
so many different digital asset opportunities that you might feel
overwhelmed. Truthfully, it's a full-time job being immersed in
digital asset investing. And for that reason, we're going to see the
emergence of digital asset advisors and managers in the coming
years. In the same way that many of us broker our investments
out to people or companies who can manage our money full-
time, we'll have digital asset managers that take care of our
Metaverse asset portfolio. The irony is that this job likely won't

be filled by your traditional financial advisor. Rather, this job role will be led by people you'd never imagine managing your money.

NFTs have become a financial vehicle with many different businesses productizing this asset class. We've already seen NFT-backed loans come into existence with Pawnfi and NFTfi. We've already seen protocols created for securely renting and loaning NFTs to complete strangers with ReNFT. So why would it be unfair to assume that the Metaverse won't have financial planners who manage digital assets on our behalf?

Overall, the wide world of Metaverse assets is an opportunity prime for the taking. It comes with risk, a lot of future-thinking, and a level of technical understanding that you should not gloss over. Because if you lose the keys to your house, you can always call a locksmith to let you in. But if you lose the keys to your blockchain wallet, then you'll never get into your "metahome."

CHAPTER

8

Challenges of the Metaverse

If *Snow Crash* introduced us to the Metaverse and *Ready Player, One* previewed the expansiveness of Metaverse economies, then *Ralph Breaks the Internet* showed us what an interoperable Metaverse looks like. The second movie in the *Wreck-It Ralph* series, *Ralph Breaks the Internet* beautifully visualizes many of the basic features of the Internet from how search engines work to how viruses spread. After Ralph unintentionally causes his best friend Venellope's game to break rendering her "jobless" and homeless, the pair venture into the Internet to buy the part off eBay needed to fix the arcade game. At this point, the movie shows us what it means to earn money on the Internet, from video game bounties to going viral and earning ad revenue.

However, what truly makes this movie special is the way they approach interoperability and the ability to easily meander between digital experiences. In our minds, this is what the Metaverse looks like—effortlessly porting between a video game into YouTube then into a search engine into a digital library.

Furthermore, it gives a concrete vision for how our favorite Internet companies may be experienced as Metaverse environments in the future.

Achieving this seamless version of the Metaverse is easier said than done. Interoperability is the primary hurdle here. It's the basis for most of the challenges preventing the Metaverse vision we've described throughout this book from coming true. An open Metaverse is what we're all striving for after all. Not a bunch of disparate, closed gardens. If there isn't interoperability in our assets, payments, and ability to move between platforms, then we're not actually innovating, and we may as well stick with the current video games, social experiences, and Internet infrastructure that we have today.

Perhaps the largest of these interoperability challenges is making all of the Metaverse economies, assets, and currencies cooperate.

Interoperable Economies

Metaverse users need to be able to carry their digital valuables from one gaming or social Metaverse to another. As the world stands today with payments in gaming, the current systems are not conducive to the Metaverse. If you spend money on V-Bucks (*Fortnite*'s currency), you can never convert it back into dollars. Furthermore, V-Bucks cannot be converted into Robux on *Roblox*. We're not saying that anything is inherently wrong with these "closed garden" economies. Each gaming publisher has the right to keep their currency native to their platform.

However, the vision of the Metaverse is interoperable and therefore needs payment portability between platforms. This goes for both fungible and non-fungible tokens. In other words, both the currencies we use (fungible) and the in-game assets we own (non-fungible/NFTs) need to work across Metaverses.

Fungible tokens (think Bitcoin, Ethereum, $MANA, and even the US dollar) are already interoperable. Cryptocurrency by the nature of it is portable across the Metaverse. If you are a hardcore *Axie Infinity* gamer and have earned a boatload of their $SLP tokens through gameplay, you can bring that $SLP to an exchange and leave with Bitcoin, $MANA, or any Metaverse currency you choose. It takes some time and transaction fees to convert said currency. But fungible tokens are already bringing interoperability in payments to the Metaverse.

There is a point, though, where there are too many fungible tokens in the Metaverse, thus leading to an overall worse user experience. By the looks of it now, every single gaming and sandbox Metaverse is going to have their own in-game currency. And this is a bit worrisome because we don't feel it's completely necessary. There needs to be purpose to these fungible tokens if you're going to create them. And that utility can't just be that it's the currency of their platform.

We look at a web3 company like Brave who is building a decentralized web browser. They use their Basic Attention Token (BAT) currency to power their advertising-based economy. Advertisers must purchase BAT respective to the number of ads and market of users they plan to reach. In turn, these BAT tokens are paid out to the users who have the ad pop-ups. But their currency stops there. Although BAT is the foundation of their product and service, largely incentivizing their user base to use the browser instead of Chrome, it lacks any further utility. We want to see them offer NFT-based upgrades where users can spend their BAT on a VPN upgrade, maybe a Brave chat feature, or other simple Internet services that could easily be native to the Brave browser.

This is a position that we see so many Metaverse companies repeating, where their token fuels their economy but all users can do is earn the token, spend the token, vote using the token, or convert the token to another crypto. This would be okay if that weren't the same features of every single other Metaverse platform's currency. The result is you have all of these fragmented currencies that users must consistently exchange for other currencies, ultimately causing users to spend a lot of their money on exchange fees.

There's a happy medium that we're going to have to find with respect to fungible Metaverse tokens. We'll need enough currencies to keep developer competition high, but not too many where we create friction and fragmentation that prevents users from having cross-Metaverse portability.

Where there's truthfully zero Metaverse interoperability is in non-fungible tokens, our Metaverse assets. If we're going to spend hundreds or thousands of dollars on an NFT, we should be able to bring that asset into any of the blockchain-based Metaverses. That is not our reality today, though. Our Axies cannot be brought into Decentraland. Our Bored Apes have no place on the current Metaverse platforms. There's very little asset interplay between Metaverses.

We admire MetaMundo's approach to this problem. On their marketplace, every 3D NFT asset you purchase comes with a bundle of files of that NFT in a variety of file formats to fit each major sandbox Metaverse. Their process centers around a parent-child NFT structure, whereby the NFT asset in its highest resolution and original intention is the parent file. That parent file gives the owner access to download that NFT's child files that are the numerous iterations of that NFT in Metaverse-supported file formats such as .vox, .vrm, .obj, and so on.

To anyone who is looking to design and sell 3D NFTs for the Metaverse, this is currently the best way to ensure that your NFT is going to be Metaverse agnostic and thus interoperable across the future Metaverse landscape. Aside from file type, though, we also have to think about the many different blockchains the

Metaverse is being built on from the Ethereum chain to Solana to Flow and many more. Currently, if you want to take an NFT from one blockchain to another, you can use a blockchain bridge like Portal by Wormhole. The Konvoy VC firm outlines the problems with this current process as such:

> "These bridges do not enable actual transfer and are not a true acknowledgment of value and ownership across chains. The asset is not literally moved from one chain to another. Instead, the assets are frozen in smart contracts and a new version is minted on the other chain."

At the moment, a cross-chain asset is nothing more than a copy of the original asset. Although only one can exist at a time, either the original or copy on another blockchain, this leaves a lot of room for exploitable loopholes when the smart contract does not explicitly state transferability conditions. Overall, portability of Metaverse assets across file types and across blockchains is a major challenge for the interoperable Metaverse.

You might be thinking, "Wouldn't Metaverse asset interoperability shrink the overall market for these assets and ultimately be less lucrative for game and Metaverse developers?" If you can buy a hoodie in Decentraland and convert it to a hoodie that also works in The Sandbox, then isn't that one less digital hoodie that you're going to buy? That's exactly what we're stating because that's how the real world works. When you buy a new suit for an upcoming wedding, that suit doesn't stop being a suit when you dress up for your niece's graduation.

This idea of interoperable assets gets quite tricky when it comes to gaming assets. Guns in *Call of Duty* have features programmed into them that do not make sense in *Fortnite*. To use a gaming Metaverse example, an NFT spacecraft in *Star Atlas* has underlying specs that are an entirely different feature set from the NFT spacecraft in *Alien Worlds*. While we'd like to imagine that these NFT gaming assets people are spending absurd amounts of money on will eventually work in other Metaverse games, the coordination required would be immense. There's a huge opportunity for gaming Metaverses to partner with one another and coordinate the features of their assets. At the minimum, there can be a compromise where outside assets can be brought into a gaming Metaverse (or any Metaverse platform) and at least show the cosmetic features. So if the Jadu Jetpack in The Sandbox gives us the ability to fly, the least that Decentraland can do is allow us to wear the jetpack (even if it doesn't give us flight there). It's an optimistic outlook, for sure. But an outlook we'd like to believe in.

We realize that technology doesn't always get built with the user's best interest in mind. However, to have a Metaverse that is truly best for the user, the companies and developers behind these projects must change their mindset. The idea that a game's economy will only exist in that game is not conducive to the Metaverse. The idea that developers have to build and sell everything in-house is being replaced by the decentralized mindset of other people helping build out the assets and experiences in your game or social space.

Also, an interoperable Metaverse economy doesn't mean that platforms will ultimately lose out. We've already seen a taste of this play out on OpenSea. You don't have to go to Decentraland or The Sandbox marketplaces to buy land. You can get them right on OpenSea where the vast majority of NFT shopping is done. And the smart contracts are written in such a way where Decentraland and The Sandbox still get their cut of the transaction when it's sold there. The Metaverse mindset must be one where everyone has a chance to eat at the dinner table. And Metaverse assets and economies at large must have portability and compatibility in mind.

Interoperable Graphics and Hardware

Closely related to interoperable Metaverse economies are the graphics and hardware used to access the Metaverse. We've addressed that file types are a barrier to carrying assets between Metaverses. But the graphics of each Metaverse is entirely different too, and thus a challenge to consider.

For example, video games rarely have the same visual DNA. *Roblox* and *Minecraft* are visually similar in their blocky characters and environments. However, *Fortnite* is more like a mix of realism, cartoons, and anime. Furthermore, *Call of Duty* and *NBA 2k* have consistently pushed graphics to be visually similar to the real world. If you search any of the Metaverses outlined in Chapter 6, "Enter the Metaverse," it's going to take you far longer to find a visual match than it will to find two that look entirely different. Graphics are important to a game's DNA, and we're not suggesting visual hegemony between all Metaverses. That would make for a boring and unimaginative Metaverse. However, if we want Metaverse asset portability to be a thing and for us to be able to bring the billions of dollars spent on NFTs between Metaverses, then we'll need to find a way to translate the graphics of our Metaverse assets and environments.

And that brings us to hardware. Are the Metaverse hardware companies going to play nice and make interoperability a standard? We're referring to the primary gaming consoles Xbox and PlayStation, in addition to the VR companies, namely, Meta's Oculus VR headsets, HTC's headsets, and Sony PlayStation VR.

What does interoperability at the hardware level look like? First that players, no matter which hardware they're using, can coexist in Metaverse experiences. But also, that these hardware companies don't overindex on developing proprietary games and Metaverse experiences that are closed off from the other platforms, thus creating more platform disconnectedness.

Cross-hardware compatibility isn't out of the question. As we discussed in Chapter 5, "The Metaverse Building Blocks," CEO Tim Sweeney of Epic Games summarized the new thinking surrounding gaming environments. He explained the trepidation involved when *Fortnite* was connecting gamers across competing systems. Nobody initially wanted to open up their platforms to competitors. But once Xbox, PlayStation, and Switch players were able to play cross-platform, all the platforms benefited. Sweeney said, "I think everybody realizes there's a much bigger opportunity in connecting people than keeping people apart."

Metaverse adoption and usage will only grow by connecting users across devices. Obviously, Epic Games is in the software business, but we feel his view should be (and will be) shared by the gaming hardware companies as well when it comes to the Metaverse. It won't come without hurdles, though. After all, we're talking about crossbreeding competing revenue streams.

Just look at the legal battle between Epic Games and Apple. In Epic Games' quest to connect their *Fortnite* users across all devices, they're being gouged by Apple App Store's 30 percent tax on all in-game transactions. Considering that *Fortnite*'s entire revenue is based around players buying in-game assets, Epic Games contends that it doesn't make financial sense for them to support Apple devices anymore. Of course, this case will dictate the future of the App Store's business model, which grossed somewhere between $70 and $80 billion USD in 2021 according to CNBC.

The point here is that hardware and software compatibility won't come without financial battles. And if these partnerships don't feel that the dollars make "cents," then we could see Metaverse fragmentation at the foundational device level.

We wish that we had a confident take on how this will all play out. There's the future we'd like to see and the future that's more likely. With Meta basing the lion's share of their future on VR and the Metaverse, we unfortunately don't see them being open to this interoperable Metaverse. On the other hand, PlayStation has their own VR headset and Xbox does not. If Xbox wants to compete in VR, then an exclusive partnership with Meta's Oculus platform wouldn't be out of the question.

As you can see, solving for Metaverse's future interoperability is not going to be easy. Incompatibility between Metaverses will be the standard long before interoperability is a thing. Although we see it as the greatest challenge facing the Metaverse becoming something great, this is unfortunately not the only challenge that the Metaverse faces.

The Negative Narratives of the Metaverse

Change is not easy, especially when it challenges everything we know to be true about what we trust in, care for, and associate value to. The Metaverse introduces many new concepts that are not easily understood. From digital ownership to virtual presence, the Metaverse is based in changing our relationship with the Internet and digital livelihood. And with these changes come narratives working against this new idea.

Starting with the most popular of all negative narratives would be the aura surrounding NFTs. This technology that brought about the idea of digital scarcity and true digital asset ownership has gotten quite the bad wrap. Many people view these digital collectibles as a scam. They are routinely dragged through the mud for the occasional rug pull and cash grab, despite there being real builders there with plans for utility and longevity. We believe that the learning curve of blockchain that is necessary to participating in this market has contributed greatly to these negative narratives. After all, people tend to talk poorly about that which they don't understand. Considering digital ownership and thus NFTs are a big part of the Metaverse, a lot of education will be needed to get over this hump of misunderstanding.

Another underlying Metaverse technology not in the best graces in the public eye is virtual reality. Although the consumer interest has come a long way in the past few years, virtual reality in general is not a super-appealing technology. A general sentiment shared by many (including Elon Musk) is that as kids we were once told not to sit too close to the TV, and now we're strapping them a couple inches from our eyes. Jaron Lanier, one of the pioneers of virtual reality, says that VR should be the device of our dreams but could end up being the device of nightmares by leading us down a path of major behavior modification. Dystopian visions of people becoming too reliant on virtual existence come a dime a dozen. Not to mention, when Facebook revealed a few VR-related patents that would give the Oculus headset the ability to track our emotions, it obviously struck a chord with people. With any new technology there is always going to be the potential for a negative behavioral shift. Most of us didn't foresee that happening with smartphones, but it did occur in many ways. As for virtual reality, it's simply easier to foresee those negative impacts on life, while ignoring the positive outcomes.

And the last major narrative working against the Metaverse is that it's all about gaming. Because companies like *Roblox*, *Fortnite*, and *Minecraft* are routinely looked at as early iterations of the Metaverse, it's easy to associate the Metaverse with video games. Virtual reality propagates this idea a lot, as you'll often see Meta's Oculus headset commercials prominently featuring video games. And *Ready Player, One*, whether you read the book or watched the movie, showcased a Metaverse that is inspired almost entirely by video game culture. In reality, professional communication, collaboration, and community building are some of the most important features that Metaverse companies are building. Regardless, the Metaverse will need to circumvent this narrative that it's a gaming concept.

And as we explored in Chapter 7, "Metaverse Assets," concern has also been expressed about bad actors who have attempted to exploit the Metaverse and unscrupulously game the investment climate. But as we discussed there, investigators and watchdogs are already evolving to help address those situations.

Overall, this chapter might make you feel as though there's a lot more working against the Metaverse than there is working for it. How we handle the platform differences in currencies, hardware, assets, graphics, etc., are not easy challenges, for sure. But when we think about a true Metaverse experience that a lot of people, not just us, dream of, it has to be interoperable. Otherwise, the Metaverse is just not all that compelling. If it's not interoperable, then the only innovation is ownership and digital earning potential. And guess what? *Fortnite* can do that if they want to. *Roblox* can build an asset resale marketplace and ways to earn Robux in the game without the blockchain.

Ultimately, the blockchain is the glue, the connector that makes Metaverse interoperability work. It's going to take time to solve these challenges and build systems that make sense. But we're bullish on the builders coming into this space, in addition to all of the people and companies who are betting their lives on this vision coming to fruition.

9

Your Metaverse Plan

Not long ago, we read an article about a man who had driven his car past the million-mile mark. In a little over three decades, Jim O'Shea managed to keep his same Volvo operating and pass the monumental milestone with ease. He was inspired to do so after hearing about another man by the name of Irv Gordon, who had driven his 1966 Volvo past that benchmark by 1993 (and continued to a record of 3.2 million miles). Like most people, we've never even considered owning a car that long, let alone racking up that many miles without any major accidents. However, the idea got us thinking.

What device or technology do we use today that could pass the (metaphorical) million-mile mark?

Believe us, we racked our brains for a while on this thought prompt. Outside of maybe an analog watch, a few well-made kitchen appliances, and certain retro video game consoles, consumer technology usually doesn't go the distance. At least on the hardware side of things. But as far as software goes, there are numerous technologies that have surpassed their million miles of lifetime usage. Microsoft Office Suite, HTTPS, Google Search, file formats, Linux OS...the list goes on.

Even as this software evolves, we have the ability to bridge the old standards with the new. And that's how we feel about the Metaverse today. The Metaverse is a software, and we're only at version 1. It's challenging to see what version 2 looks like and downright impossible to see what version 3 may hold. But that doesn't mean you cannot approach the Metaverse with plans to surpass the million virtual mile mark. Longevity in the Metaverse deemphasizes immediate revenue while prioritizing building your Metaverse spaces, gathering your community, and contributing to this environment in novel ways.

Whichever way you choose to involve yourself or your company in the Metaverse, first ask yourself if this plan will last a million virtual miles.

Designing Your Metaverse Plan

By now, if you don't think the Metaverse is a real opportunity or you don't see the power of virtual economies, then either we've done our job incorrectly or you just haven't yet reached your aha moment. And we're not upset about that. The Metaverse represents many major shifts to how we operate today. It's a lot to digest. So even though we believe the Metaverse is one of the most extraordinary developments to happen in the last several decades and are aligning a lot of our interests toward this virtual world, we realize that not everyone is ready for that commitment just yet.

At a fundamental level, the Metaverse is a new way to learn, connect, and share culture. No matter whether you're a decision-maker at a brand or corporation with significant intellectual property (IP), an entertainer seeking the next marketing channel, or simply an Interest Geek looking to get involved in the digital landscape, there are many ways to dip your toes in the Metaverse waters.

What you've manifested and cultivated in the past is not dead, but it's also not guaranteed to work in the Metaverse. But if we were in your strategy meetings and offering up our advice on kicking off your Metaverse plans, then there are three ways we'd go about it.

For Brands and Corporations with IP

Not every brand or corporation has the cultural pull to make it in the Metaverse without creating a launchpad of sorts. You have to be honest with yourself. Is your brand or company at the caliber of Disney or LVMH? More often than not, the answer to that question is no. This means you cannot create in the dark, drop an NFT or Metaverse environment, and expect everyone to notice. There's too much happening in the Metaverse to expect that you will be the center of attention, even if for a moment.

But you have an unfair advantage that Disney and LVMH don't have. You have a community of customers, followers, and partners that most likely don't know the first thing about the Metaverse. Therefore, you can be the vector through which they learn about this stuff. You've already shown that you're a self-learner by picking up this book. Share what you're learning with your existing community. You have the power to connect with those people in a way that a Disney character, CryptoPunk, or a Decentraland cannot and has not been able to. Your existing community is your launchpad into the Metaverse. These will be your first users. But you have to be able to share your journey with them and get them to buy into what you're building.

Leaning into educating your own community has to be your superpower here. Approach this from a place of honesty. Tell them what clicked in your head that made the Metaverse make sense to you. Share what worries you still. You've already built trust among your customers, followers, and partners. You don't want to lose that trust by being as polarizing and definite as we are in this book. However, starting from an area of honest education won't tarnish your reputation.

Everyone needs to learn the basics of blockchain, digital wallets, and how to manage one's own digital assets at some point. The world cannot rely only on futuristic techie voices like us. After all, we usually sound like beings from another planet. But you know what will drive the point home to your community. You know the analogies and mental models that will help this stuff make sense because you know their pain points better than we do. Your goal should be to help share that aha moment with your community because if you are the vector at which they come to understand this stuff, then they'll buy into whatever you end up building.

After you've spent some time building that knowledge base amongst your community, then you can focus on constructing your Metaverse plans. At this point, begin thinking about what you want to uniquely offer the world. What is the value that your brand or company is known for? Why do people respect your product or service? What benefit do you provide your users? Lean into answering these questions first, as this will determine which valuable IP of yours will translate to the Metaverse.

The Sears Towers in Chicago is iconic. Even though the name was officially changed to the Willis Tower in 2009, Chicagoans (and the entire world, for that matter) still refer to it as the Sears Tower. If we were leading Metaverse strategy for Sears, guess what we're going to build in The Sandbox or Decentraland?

Land in the Metaverse is new and likely the cheapest it will ever be. A great first place to start as a brand or corporation is simply attaching your company to a plot of land in the Metaverse and building around that. We're going to experience the Metaverse around locations. In the Metaverse's infinite vastness, we're going to memorize these maps by points of interest. Users will tell their friends, "Hey, meet me at Kohl's Plaza." Or, "Yo, I'm hanging out at the Land O' Lakes Lounge, come through." You can start small by building a social space like Benny Or did with The Meeting Place.

And it doesn't just have to be in The Sandbox or Decentraland if you're priced out of that land. Go back and reread Chapter 6, "Enter the Metaverse." There are so many Metaverse worlds to build in, whether it's a sandbox Metaverse or a gaming Metaverse. And because many of these Metaverses exist on the blockchain, you have that transparency to see what the traffic and user bases are like and can let data power your decisions.

This holds true especially if your company has traditionally existed in one dimension or has not really seen itself as a tech-forward company. Now is the best time to reinvent oneself in the digital dimension. Now is the time to reimagine your brand's value in a new format. And these time investments in the Metaverse today are going to pay great compounding returns.

For example, look at a company like BlackBerry, which everyone largely recognizes as a failed smartphone company that was put to bed by Apple. But a lot of people don't know that when it comes to automotive operating systems, it's BlackBerry versus Tesla. It's not widely talked about that BlackBerry's QNX operating system is the preferred choice for some of the largest automakers today including BMW, Ford, GM, Honda, Mercedes-Benz, Toyota, and Volkswagen. They're literally impacting hundreds of millions of people on a daily basis. Although BlackBerry lost the battle over smartphones, it quietly reinvented itself and found a new battle to fight.

So even if you feel that your brand or company has missed out on the Web2 era, the social Internet, or the TikTok movement, you're not counted out from realizing success in the Web3 era.

We'd recommend that you pick up a copy of *The NFT Handbook* (Wiley 2021) and start familiarizing yourself with NFTs and digital assets. Gather your IP and define your unique advantages. Figure out what pieces you're missing on the tech side (or the design side) and start to build in public.

Above all, don't forget about the customers, followers, and partners who already rock with you and help bring them up to speed. They are your ultimate launch pad to entering the Metaverse with style and grace.

For Entertainers

If you are an entertainer or are associated with the entertainment business, then you're already in a great position to carve out your space in the Metaverse. You might have a talent or domain expertise that you can share in the Metaverse. You probably have some important IP or content that can be re-created in the Metaverse.

If we were in your position, then we'd start in the area of digital twins, which you will recall from Chapter 5, "The Building Blocks of the Metaverse." Your digital twin can be an ever-present reflection of you or even a spokesperson for your brand. Your digital twin can be a virtual recreation of your best stand-up routine, performance, or DJ set. What this ultimately looks like is Travis Scott's Astronomical event in *Fortnite*. That was a choreographed performance where every single detail was programmed to work as they wished, and it led to Travis Scott celebrating his third No. 1 on the Billboard Hot 100 chart (dated May 9, 2020).

We're in an era where the entertainment business is hungry for Metaverse case studies to reverse engineer and learn from. Frankly, most people are scared to share their ideas because they think everyone is going to steal their IP and ideas. But honestly, if Metaverse ideas were easily stolen, then we'd be much further along than we already are. Stealing the idea is easy. Actually executing a Metaverse installation is very difficult. A lot of people have rushed into NFTs and the Metaverse without taking the time to make it great. This is not a race. We look at the mad dash among celebrities to mint NFTs back in the summer of 2021. Many of those who rushed into it, just trying to "NFT their likeness" in any way, are no longer around. They are washed up and not trusted (by digital collectors) anymore because they clearly were after the hype and the money. So take your time and be thoughtful.

Most likely, the hardest part for you will be translating your ideas into the technical requirements of the Metaverse. So first continue to educate yourself on the concepts discussed in this book and *The NFT Handbook*. Then start to sketch out your ideas. It can be as simple as "I want to do X. I think I'm missing this piece. And I may need help from that type of person." Then don't be afraid to have conversations to find the people that can help you build your vision.

If you're still stuck and need help, you know that DJ SKEE (one of the authors of this book) has been building Metaverse installations for several years. Notably, you might have heard that he and his company DASH helped Paris Hilton create her digital twin in the Metaverse by building Paris World in *Roblox*. Feel free to reach out to his team at https://dxsh.mv.

For Metaverse Interest Geeks

For all of you Metaverse Interest Geeks, it's never been a better time to build the "Metaverse for X." What communities are you part of? What interests do you have that don't yet exist in the Metaverse?

We're going to reach a point in time where every niche culture, every interest, and every single sub-Reddit group has a digital equivalent in the Metaverse. You can be the agent who sparks the Metaverse movement of your interest. We look at an NFT-based project called Club CPG that essentially took their love of consumer packaged goods and built an exclusive mentorship community around that interest. Their mission has grown and even caught the attention of Mark Cuban, who is now one of the mentors in that community.

The history of the Internet is one that is flush with stories of niche communities doing great things. *50 Shades of Grey* was originally written in periodic installments on various *Twilight* fan-fiction websites. The popular workplace chat app Slack was actually spun out of a failed MMO game called *Glitch*.

If you're an Interest Geek, be the coordinator who starts putting the wheels in motion for a Metaverse that fits your shared interest. You don't have to tackle this all by yourself. There are plenty of Metaverse Interest Geeks who will build and market alongside you. If you're worried about it growing bigger than you and losing a place in the space, then learn a unique and advantageous skill like Unity or Blender. Make yourself indispensable.

There's going to be a massive trend around the idea of "the Metaverse for X." By already showing up and beginning the learning process, you're well-positioned to be one of the Metaverse Interest Geeks who will build something great.

Further Reading at MetaverseQT.com

As we draw this book to a close, we want to first thank you for purchasing *The Metaverse Handbook* and showing interest in this new virtual paradigm. We know that the concepts are not easy and seem to be changing every month. Ultimately, this book is a time capsule of what we know about the Metaverse, how we understand it, and what we envision the future will hold at the time that we're publishing this book. While we've done our best to create a resource that will stand the test of time, inevitably some of what we've written will be rendered obsolete by the evolutions of the coming years.

That's why we've created an ongoing resource to share what's happening in the Metaverse. We'll be covering the new companies that emerge, outlining creator case studies, and documenting the overall progress of the Metaverse in real-time. So if you're hungry for more Metaverse insights, research, and tips, please head over to https://MetaverseQT.com.

And of course, feel free to connect with us, QuHarrison Terry (@QuHarrison) and Scott "DJ SKEE" Keeney (@DJSKEE), any time and any place you can find us on the Internet. We're eager to hear what you think of the book, any Metaverse ideas you have, and where you believe this industry is going.

Until next time, we'll catch you in the Metaverse.

Index